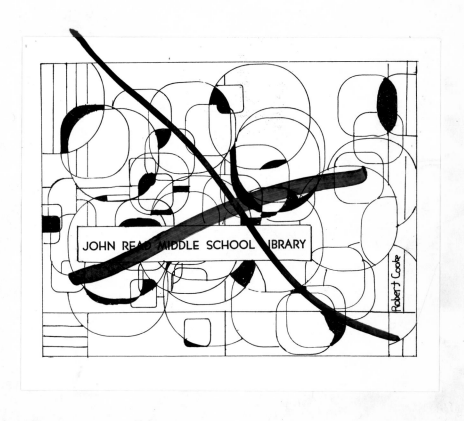

Peggy Fleming
Cameo of a Champion

Peggy Fleming

McGraw-Hill Book Company

New York   St. Louis   San Francisco
Auckland   Bogotá   Düsseldorf
Johannesburg   London   Madrid
Mexico   Montreal   New Delhi
Panama   Paris   São Paulo
Singapore   Sydney   Tokyo   Toronto

Cameo of a Champion

by Elizabeth Van Steenwyk

illustrated with photographs

Library of Congress Cataloging in Publication Data

Van Steenwyk, Elizabeth.
Peggy Fleming: cameo of a champion.

Includes index.
Summary: A biography of the figure skater who
was the only American to win a gold medal at the
1968 winter Olympics and the youngest skater to be
inducted into skating's Hall of Fame in 1975.
1. Fleming, Peggy—Juvenile literature.   2. Skaters—
United States—Biography—Juvenile literature.
[1. Fleming, Peggy. 2. Ice skaters] I. Title
GV850.F55V36   796.9'1'0924   [92]   77-17060
ISBN 0-07-067167-2

Designed by Suzanne Haldane

1 2 3 4 5 6 7 8 9   B P B P   7 8 3 2 1 0 9 8

Contents

The author gratefully acknowledges the assistance of William Udell, photographer, performer and coach of figure skating; friend of the novice as well as the pro.

Foreword by Peggy Fleming

Skating always has been an important part of my life and I am grateful for what it taught me. First, I learned to discipline mind and body in compulsory school figures. Accepting responsibility when I represented my country in competition was another valuable lesson. Finally, the challenge of self-expression in the interpretive free-style events made me aware of my own potential at a far earlier age than would have been true without skating.

But there is danger in concentrating so hard on only one activity in life at so early an age. It can engulf, even smother, other worthwhile goals. Fortunately, I was blessed with parents and coaches who helped me see all of my life in proper perspective. As they taught me to do my best in skating, they also encouraged me to discover other outlets . . . other goals. Therefore, I practiced, studied and competed in skating as best I could. But I also learned along the way that my best applied to academics in school, making friends and being one, becoming a professional performer, a wife and a parent.

I guess you can say, then, that skating taught me to be true to the best that's within me in whatever I'm involved. I hope the story of my life will show you what I mean. As you are growing up, I hope you'll discover, just as I did, your own goals . . . your own dreams . . . your own values.

Always give the best that's in you.

Love,

Peggy Fleming Jenkins

Peggy Fleming
Cameo of a Champion

1

Where Did It Begin?

On the evening of February 10, 1968, Peggy Fleming sat in a dressing room assigned to her and two other American girls, located deep in the cavernous Stade de Glace in Grenoble, France. She looked at herself carefully in the mirror and then combed her dark hair again. Then she walked to the closet and examined her skating costume of pale green jersey, edged with sparkling rhinestones at the neck and cuffs. Finally, Peggy touched the place where she'd pinned the lucky green gum wrapper inside her costume. It was there, safe and secure. She thought of Greg, who had given it to her, and smiled.

"What number did you draw, Peggy?" Tina Noyes asked, lacing her boots.

"Twenty-two." Peggy returned to her chair and sat

down before the mirror. She wondered if it was too soon to put on eye shadow.

"Wow," Janet Lynn said. "You've got a long wait."

Peggy smiled as she looked at Tina and Janet, the other two skaters representing the United States. She knew only too well that she would have to wait a long time before skating. She would have to stay here while twenty-one girls from other countries skated in the free-style portion of the Olympic competition tonight. Finally, her turn would come. Then ten more girls would skate after her. At least she wasn't last.

"I don't know which is best." Tina brushed her red hair away from her face. "Skate early and get it over with, or skate later and know what your competitors have done."

Janet shook her head solemnly. "Either way, it's hard."

"One thing for sure," Tina said. "We don't have much choice in the matter."

As Peggy lost herself in thought, tuning out Tina's and Janet's quiet conversation, she tried not to bite her lips and tense her shoulders to display the nervousness she felt.

Think of it as just another competition, Peggy, she thought. Or, better yet, as just another practice session. She'd been landing the jumps during every practice lately, especially since winning the Nationals in Philadelphia last month. She had never skated so well in her life as during that competition.

But her attempt at self-deception didn't work. Even playing mental tricks with herself, she just couldn't escape the overwhelming thing soon to take place. Peggy just couldn't ignore the importance of these next few hours. Keep your head together, she thought.

Competition is not exactly a new experience, Peggy reminded herself, checking her makeup carefully. After all, she'd been skating since she was nine years old and winning since she was ten. But tonight was special, the competition she'd dreamed about, waited for during all those long, meticulous hours of practice on the ice. This was the Winter Olympics, 1968, and she was poised, ready and waiting now, for the most important event of her nineteen years. Would she win and have her name written in the Olympic record books? Soon now, she'd know and so would the rest of the world.

Tina checked her blade guards and walked slowly to the door.

"Good luck, Tina," Peggy said smiling.

Janet looked up, her short blonde hair capping her pixie face. "Yeah, Tina. Good luck."

"Thank you," Tina said, and moved down the hall toward the arena.

After a moment's hesitation, Janet stood up. "I can't sit still. Think I'll go watch." She clumped out, her skate guards thudding on the rubber-tiled floor.

Peggy thought about all the television cameras that soon would be focused on Tina to send her performance around the world and home to the United States via early-bird satellite. In a couple of hours, they would be focused on her. What would those cameras show the world, she wondered. What would they tell about her?

She sat back in her chair and tried to relax, but her

thoughts whirled on, gliding first in one direction, then another. Finally, she gave in to them.

If she won tonight, Peggy thought, she would be the first athlete from the United States to earn a gold medal during this Olympiad and the first American figure skater to win since 1960. Yes, she would be winning for her country and herself, but for others, too. In a way, that medal would belong to a lot of people. Her mother, now seated somewhere in the stadium, and her sisters, Janice, Maxine and Cathy, back home in Colorado, deserved their share. And Dad, Peggy thought. A part of the gold medal will belong to Dad's memory, if I win. Dad's help was so special, she hardly knew how to frame it in words. Let's see, she thought. Then slowly, ever so slowly, the words formed in her mind: Dad taught me to always do my best and, above all, to enjoy it.

She felt someone touching her arm and looked up, startled, to see her coach, Carlo Fassi, smiling at her. His dark eyes were brilliant in the glare of the dressing-room lights.

"Just a little while longer, Peggy."

"And then all the waiting and worrying will be over."

"Look, if you don't feel like doing the second double axel, don't do it," Carlo said.

"I'll see, when the time comes."

"Okay." He touched her arm again. "I'll be waiting by the door to the ice when it's your turn." He smiled and was gone, knowing her need to be alone now.

When did all this begin, she asked herself. Was there a time she could remember when she didn't know how to skate? Yes, but it seemed to be a time primarily of skinned knees and scraped elbows. Funny, she thought, smiling to herself. When I started skating, I had fewer accidents.

But when did it start, she thought. When did I actually begin to skate? She looked deep into her memory well. Oh, yes, now I remember. It was in Cleveland, when I was nearly nine. We lived there for awhile, when Dad was learning his trade as a newspaper pressman. That's when all this really began.

2

Early Days in Cleveland

*P*eggy removed her violin from its case and put it under her chin. Her sister Janice had practiced earlier and now it was Peggy's turn. Although her teacher and Mom said she had natural ability, Peggy hated playing and liked to get the practicing over as quickly as possible. Maybe, if she stood close to the open dining-room door and played real loud, Mom and Dad would tell her to stop. Maybe then she'd have time to go back outdoors and play in the warm autumn twilight.

Peggy dawdled over her exercises while listening to her folks' voices in the living room, and watching them through the doorway. She was prepared to quit at the slightest lift of her Dad's eyebrow or glance her way.

Mom had settled down in a favorite chair to sip a cup of after-dinner coffee. "Peggy has more accidents than the other three girls put together," she heard Mom say over her squeaky music.

"She's an active little girl for sure," Dad said. "Always hanging upside down from a tree limb or playing football with the neighbor kids." Peggy saw Dad turn to the sports section of the newspaper. Once he'd participated actively in sports, but due to a World War II–related illness, he now could only be a spectator.

Mom smiled as she patted a wisp of dark brown hair into place. "Today she scraped her knees on her scooter," Mom said. "Yesterday she needed stitches on her chin. "It's always something."

So far they hadn't seemed to notice her violin playing. She stopped now and carefully examined her bow.

Dad put his newspaper down. "It isn't lack of coordination that's the problem," he said. "She has more than most kids her age."

"I think the problem is her energy. She has more of that than most kids her age, too." Mom laughed as she spoke those words. "The trips to the zoo are fun and the art lessons at the museum for all the girls are interesting, especially for Maxine."

"But Peggy needs . . . " Dad began and stopped to search for the right words.

"Peggy needs something to do that will make use of her excess reserve of energy," Mom finished.

"Sounds like you've got something in mind," Dad said. He put down the paper to smile at Mom. His dark, almost black, hair shone in the lamplight.

"Remember how she loved to skate the few times we took all the girls to the ice rink in California when we lived in Walnut Creek?"

"That was fun," he said. "Especially for Peggy."

"She didn't fall once," Mom said. Dad's blue-green eyes crinkled up as he laughed. Then she continued. "There's an indoor ice rink like it in downtown Cleveland. I'll take her there tomorrow and see what happens."

"Good idea," Dad said as Peggy squeaked through her final violin exercise. "Then maybe she won't have so much time to practice the violin."

Whoopee, Peggy thought, putting her violin away. Ice skating's a lot more fun than this.

The following day after school, Mom put little sister Cathy in the car and then drove Peggy to the rink. A blast of chilly air greeted them as they walked through the front door. She shivered slightly as she laced on the boots of the skates they'd rented, but it was probably more from excitement than the cold air. Then Peggy stepped out on the ice and stroked hesitantly, carefully, at first. Skating in California those few times hadn't really given her much opportunity to find her skating legs.

Gradually, her strokes grew longer and she completed several circles around the rink with the other skaters. And she didn't fall, didn't feel as if she would ever fall! Skating wasn't difficult, it was fun! More fun than riding a bicycle or running a race or, especially, playing that violin! She peeled off a jacket the next time around the ice and handed it to Mom, and the next time around a sweater. As she began to relax, she became aware of the music playing over the loudspeaker and tried to time her strokes to the music. There, now she was keeping time to that waltz. She knew it was a waltz because of the one-two-three counting business her violin teacher made her do. Around and around she went, losing herself in the rhythmic movement of her legs in time to the music.

When the record was finished, the announcer's voice boomed out over the loudspeaker. "Couples only. Couples only, skating next."

Reluctantly, Peggy skated off and threw herself into a rinkside seat beside Mom and Cathy.

"Are you thirsty?" Mom looked up from her knitting.

"No, thank you. I just want to skate."

Peggy watched the boys in bright Nordic sweaters and girls in short skating dresses and tights as they skated around and around the rink. She knew they were having fun, but she wished this part would hurry up. She thumped her skates impatiently on the rubber-tiled floor.

An older girl, with long blonde hair caught up in a ponytail, stopped near them to watch the skaters too. Peggy noticed the girl's gleaming white boots on shiny skate blades. She really must be good to wear skates like that, Peggy thought. Suddenly the girl turned around and Peggy saw the name pin fastened to her collar. It spelled out Karen.

"Hi," she said. "Guess you already know my name. What's yours?"

"I'm Peggy, and this is my mom."

"You're new around here, aren't you?" Karen's brown eyes were warm and friendly.

"Yes, but I want to come back every day." Peggy

smiled up at Karen. She was so tall, she must be nearly twelve.

"Would you like to take ice-skating lessons, Peggy?" Mom asked. "Instead of violin lessons?" Mom's blue eyes twinkled as Peggy reached out to hug her.

"Oh, yes," Peggy said. "Where can we find a teacher?"

"I'm going to take a lesson in half an hour," Karen said. "Maybe you'd like to talk to my teacher. Her name is Harriet Lapish."

Later, Peggy watched Cathy while Mom visited with Mrs. Lapish. Soon it was arranged for lessons to begin the following Thursday.

After that, Thursday became Peggy's favorite day. First, she liked Mrs. Lapish, who had a gentle voice to match her manner, but most of all, she loved learning the technique of skating correctly. As Mrs. Lapish gracefully demonstrated, Peggy learned there were inside and out-side edges to the blades of her skate. Then Peggy practiced skating forward and backward on them with long strokes to build up speed. Soon her teacher taught Peggy to glide in spirals and do simple spins and jumps.

Peggy came to the rink every day to practice what Mrs. Lapish taught her. The sit-spin soon became her favorite. She would spin as fast as she could, then bend one knee and crouch down, continuing to spin on that leg close to the ice, with her free leg straight out in front of her. Once in awhile she lost control and sat down hard on the seat of her pants. Once she slid all the way across the ice, to stop at the feet of a startled teenage boy, who reached down and helped her up. But those times were few.

One Thursday, Mrs. Lapish said, "Today, we'll learn

the circle eight. Just remember that all the figures you'll ever learn to skate will be a variation based on the simplest figure eight."

Peggy watched as Mrs. Lapish skated it, then she followed. It seemed easy enough, but she wobbled a few times and skated on the flat of her blade before she got it right. Then the waltz eight came next and with each day's practice it looked better and better.

Six weeks later, Mrs. Lapish said, "I think you're ready for the Preliminary test, Peggy."

"What's that?"

"It's the beginning of a series of tests which the United States Figure Skating Association uses to judge the abilities of figure skaters. These are skaters like you, Peggy, who want to improve themselves and perhaps, one day, compete in national and international competitions."

"Like the Olympics?" Peggy asked.

"That's right. Our skaters in last year's Olympics all started just as you are beginning now, with the Preliminary test."

"That sounds awfully important. I don't think I could do that."

Mrs. Lapish smiled and then said, "We'll take it one step at a time, Peggy, but I have a feeling you can do just about anything you want to."

The day of the test arrived and Peggy awoke to a stomach full of butterflies. Nevertheless, she tried to stay calm as Mom drove her down to the rink, then sat quietly in a rinkside seat where she could watch the proceedings.

The ice had been freshly made so there was not a

blemish on it. Then it had been sectioned off with half of it reserved for the actual testing. The rest was available for patch sessions for other skaters who wanted to practice. Skaters moved out onto the testing portion of the rink now, followed by the judges bundled up in coats, hats, gloves and boots. They carried score sheets and watched closely as the skaters began their figures.

Peggy watched too, concentrating on each stroke the girl before her made. Suddenly she heard her own name called, saw Mrs. Lapish beckoning to her and knew it was her turn.

She felt nervous at first, but once she began to skate, everything else blurred in her mind. She demonstrated all eight of the skating edges, then performed a circle eight on both the outside and inside edges and finished with a waltz eight. Looking up at the judges, Peggy knew from their expressions that she'd passed and she returned their smiles with one of her own. As she began to skate off, a lady judge stopped her. Peggy liked the fur on her hat. It matched the collar of her coat.

"How old are you, Peggy?" she asked.

"Nine." She suddenly felt very shy.

"You've made a good beginning," the judge continued. "I hope we'll see more of you."

"I hope so, too," she said, and hurried home with Mom to tell Dad the news of her exciting day.

3

Meeting Mr. Turner

$\mathcal{M}$ ore exciting days followed as Peggy added another skating lesson a week to her routine. Nothing seemed more important as that time in the afternoon, now, when she slipped on her skates and glided out on to the ice. First she practiced the school figures based on the figure eight. Then she made up free style in time to the music on the loudspeaker. Peggy felt she could skate forever and it wouldn't be long enough.

One winter evening, when Peggy returned from the rink with Mom, Janice reminded her, "It's your turn to set the table tonight, Peggy."

"I did last night."

"No, I did. Tonight's my turn to wash the dishes,

unless you want to," Janice said. Her blue eyes danced teasingly.

Peggy laughed and hurried out to the kitchen to join Mom, who was preparing dinner. Her older sister knew how she hated to wash the dishes.

Just as Peggy finished setting the kitchen table, Dad opened the back door.

"Hi, honey," he said, giving her a hug and then kissing Mom, who was cooking. "I've got great news." Her sisters ran in from the living room at the sound of Dad's voice.

"What is it?" Peggy asked.

"I've finished my printing studies at the newspaper. We're going back to California. To Walnut Creek."

While Mom and her sisters erupted with excited talk about the move back home, Peggy felt strange, like a balloon that suddenly has been deflated. What was the matter with her? Of course she wanted to go home to California, but a part of her wanted to stay here, too.

"Peggy, what's wrong?" Maxine asked. Her younger sister looked at her with a worried expression in her green eyes. "Are you sick?"

"No." Peggy's voice sounded quivery. "It's just that . . . well, maybe I won't get to skate anymore. And I'll have to leave Mrs. Lapish and Karen and other kids I've met down at the rink. Maybe I'll never see them again."

"Honey, don't worry." Dad put his arm around her. "There are skating rinks in California. Don't you remember, we all went skating when we lived in Walnut Creek? And new friends can be made everywhere."

"But that rink was so far away, I probably won't get to

skate as often as I do here. And I won't know anyone. It'll be awful."

"I'll take you as many times as you want to go." Mom gave her a reassuring pat. "Before you know it, you'll feel at home there, too."

"And I'll cook dinner every night Mom drives you to the rink." Janice tried to look older than eleven. "That'll be fun."

"I'll help," Maxine volunteered. She pushed her light brown hair away from her face.

"Me, too," three-year-old Cathy said. Everyone smiled at that.

Before they left Cleveland at the end of the Christmas holidays, Peggy passed the First USFSA test with excellent marks. The three months they'd spent in Ohio while Dad studied at the *Plain Dealer* had been fun, Peggy thought, looking back in her mind. She remembered the trips to the zoo and the museum, picnics near Lake Erie, visits with cousins in nearby New York State and seeing snow for the first time. But most of all, she'd always remember learning to skate here. Skating was all she could think about now as they traveled west to Walnut Creek. She wanted to continue to skate and become better at it.

A few weeks later they were nearly settled in a house in Walnut Creek, a suburb of San Francisco. While Mom and Dad unpacked the household belongings, Peggy and her sisters straightened up their rooms and hung their clothes away in closets.

One day Peggy could wait no longer. "Now, Mom?" she asked.

"Now, Peggy." Mom laughed and hugged her close. "I've made arrangements for you to study with Eugene Turner, who teaches at Iceland in Berkeley," she said.

"Who is he?" Peggy asked.

"He's a former champion," Mom answered. "And now he's a wonderful teacher."

The following Saturday morning at six o'clock, Peggy joined twenty or so other boys and girls on the huge rink. At first everyone looked sleepy and yawned a lot while they warmed up, but soon Mr. Turner declared them ready. He picked up his microphone to direct the lesson's activities. Peggy couldn't help but notice Mr. Turner's tall, handsome appearance in his sports jacket and bow tie.

"First, we're going to work on our school figures," Mr. Turner said in his soft, pleasant voice. A couple of boys groaned. "Now, boys," Mr. Turner smiled, "you can't expect to compete unless you learn these figures. Now, let's begin. Who will demonstrate the serpentine on the left forward outside and inside edges?"

Several hands popped up and demonstrators moved out to show this figure. Then Mr. Turner explained how they could improve it and everybody worked together on his suggestions. Although Peggy knew the serpentine well, because it had been included in the First USFSA test which she'd passed in Cleveland, she practiced it over and over again. Peggy knew from her teachers and lessons that no figure could be ignored just because a test had been passed. Sometime she'd use it again.

Mr. Turner eventually made his way to each pupil and watched carefully as the figure was demonstrated.

"Good, Peggy, that's very good. Your edges are clear and sharp."

Later in the lesson, Mr. Turner directed them in figures that were new to them. These were figures they would skate in more advanced USFSA tests. After he was satisfied with this part of their lesson, Mr. Turner would announce in almost every class, "Now let's turn out the lights and see how well we can skate."

That's a real test, Peggy thought, because you can't see if your circle is too long or too wide. You can only imagine with your inner eye, as Mr. Turner calls it.

When the lights flooded the arena again, the groans went up all around her.

"Look at my circle eight," a tall boy with freckles said, pointing to the ice. "It looks more like a turtle than anything else."

"I don't want anyone to see my three," a girl named Debra said through her braces. "It looks like I used skis instead of skates."

After a short break, Mr. Turner led the way, jumping and twirling and spinning, into the free-style portion of his lesson. He encouraged them all to enjoy it as much as he did.

First they drew colored plastic chips from a hat, and then, depending on the color, they would perform a single or double or trio with some of the other kids.

Just my luck, Peggy thought. I have to skate with a boy again. Why are their hands always so sweaty?

In the fifteen minutes allotted to them, Peggy and Billy selected some records and made up a skating program to go with it. Their turn was second and they stroked out together, moving into a spiral that felt good to Peggy until Billy suddenly tripped, pulling them both down.

"I wish I was playing baseball," he mumbled, as they untangled themselves.

"I wish you were, too," Peggy replied, brushing herself off.

"That was a slow start," Mr. Turner called to them. "Let's see a fast finish."

They whirled into sit-spins that had them gasping for breath at the end. Peggy loved to spin so much that she sometimes forgot her breath gave out before her legs did.

At ten o'clock, after the lesson was over, Mom and some of the other mothers brought breakfast to the rink. Although Peggy had never liked grapefruit before, after a four-hour lesson it tasted better than a piece of chocolate cake with whipped cream.

That summer, just before Peggy's tenth birthday on July 27, Mr. Turner's pupils gave a recital at Iceland. The girls wore jersey dresses in pastel colors and the boys neat pants and shirts. Soon after that Peggy passed the Second USFSA test, and one day after class Mr. Turner called Peggy and her mother aside.

"How would you like to go to a competition, Peggy?" he asked.

"That would be fun," she said. She'd never been to one and it would be interesting to see how skaters performed in them. "Can we go, Mom?"

"Do you think you'll be ready?" Mom asked.

At first Peggy didn't understand. What did she have to do to get ready? Slowly, realization hit her. "You want me to compete?"

"I don't want you to be a spectator, Peggy," Mr. Turner laughed. Then he continued. "This is the Central Pacific competition that's going to be held at Sutro's in San Francisco. You'll enter the Juvenile Girls event and skate three figures. If you score high enough in them, you'll be asked to free skate, too."

The next day Peggy added extra practice hours to her routine. By the time competition day arrived she felt ready and eager to go.

When Peggy was called to skate her figures, she forgot everything else and worked with total concentration, thinking only of moving her body correctly and placing the figures in a precise pattern on the ice. After placing the figures, she had to trace them two more times as perfectly as possible. The rink was so quiet, Peggy could hear the grind of someone else's skate as she pushed off on a stroke.

Soon the school figures had been finished by everyone and when the scores were posted, Peggy found she had placed very well and would be asked to free skate that evening. At first she was so excited Peggy hugged everyone—Mom, her sisters, Mr. Turner and two girls she didn't even know. Then she grew quiet as she suddenly realized tonight's competition would be tougher.

She was too nervous to eat dinner and too restless to sit still doing nothing. Finally, she went to the assigned dressing room and opened the door to a room full of girls giggling and chattering to hide their fears. Peggy smiled at them, but didn't enter in their conversation. She polished her boots once more, recombed her hair into a ponytail, then put on her tights and skates, left foot first. Then she slipped into the soft, white costume with long sleeves that Mom had made especially for this evening.

At last Peggy's turn came to skate. She glided out onto the ice, waited for her recorded music to start and then moved into the program Mr. Turner choreographed for her. Her confidence grew as she realized she was skating well. Then she whirled into her final spin and skated off, bursting with happiness. This was the neatest feeling in the world. Even if she didn't win anything tonight, she'd skate again in competition, just for this feeling.

Finally, all the skaters were finished and the judges gave their scores to the announcer. He began by calling the third-place winner out on the ice. Peggy had hoped, just a little, that she might take that place, but it turned out to be someone else. Tired now, she leaned against Dad and sighed. Then the second-place winner's name was announced and she skated out on the ice to receive her prize. Peggy yawned and wanted only to go home and eat dinner and go to bed.

Then the announcer called out the name of the champion. It couldn't be. Surely she must be dreaming. Dad was shaking her gently and Maxine was shouting in her ear.

"Peggy, Peggy, are you just going to sit there?"

She skated out on the ice to receive her winner's cup and had her picture taken with the other two girls. Slowly it came to her, this warm, wonderful, winning feeling. This is what it felt like to win! Wow, it was great, just great. It was the best feeling of all. And it seemed to be so easy. Winning was the easiest thing she knew how to do.

A week later, at the Pacific Coast championships in Los

Angeles, Peggy finished last. I'll never believe winning is a snap again, she thought, as she rode home with Mom. Peggy knew her attitude had defeated her. She hadn't worked to win the way she had a week earlier. The difference between trying and not trying was the difference between first and last place. Next time she'd know better. And she knew there'd be a next time for sure. This was only the beginning.

4

Moving Up in Competition

Peggy skated with Mr. Turner for nearly a year before Dad came home and told everyone he'd been offered a better job in southern California. Although Peggy found it difficult to leave her coach, she knew that she would take his wonderful way of teaching with her. In any activity or sport she pursued—and there might be others when she entered high school in a few years—Mr. Turner's advice would always remain a part of her life.

"Perfect the basics, Peggy," Mr. Turner said on the last day. "Then use them in a free, original way as an expression of your own personality."

As soon as the family settled in a house on Marengo Street in Pasadena, Peggy walked the block and a half to the Wintergarten rink. She slipped on her skates and glided around the rink, watching some of the teachers and coaches with their pupils in the center and wondering if she'd soon be among them.

Mom came to the rink with her a few days later to sign Peggy up for lessons. She began eagerly. It wasn't long, however, until Peggy realized that her new coach's methods differed from Mr. Turner's.

"What's wrong, Peggy?" Mom called from the kitchen when Peggy came home one day earlier than usual. Peggy put her skate bag on a dining-room chair and walked slowly into the kitchen.

Peggy searched for the words that would make sense out of all her bubbling thoughts. She felt so mixed up inside.

"Let's go out and sit on the front porch to talk about it." Mom put a casserole in the oven, then she and Peggy went outside.

They sat on some porch chairs and for a few moments watched the late-afternoon traffic whiz by. The porch was partially covered by climbing vines, so they could see, yet not be seen. Peggy liked the feeling.

"Mom, my new coach is so different from Mr. Turner." There, she finally said what had been bugging her for a couple of weeks.

After a moment, Mom asked, "Wasn't Mr. Turner different from Mrs. Lapish?"

"Well, yes, that's right."

"I think you'll find each coach in skating or any other sport will have a different approach, Peggy," Mom said, with a gentleness to her voice. "Just as the way you skate will always be different from someone else's style."

"I see what you mean, Mom," Peggy said. "But sometimes, can't the difference be . . . well, so different that it makes you uncomfortable? What I mean is, somehow I don't feel at home on the ice anymore, the way I did with Mr. Turner."

Peggy watched her mother as she studied the ever-increasing traffic for a moment. Then Peggy began to worry. She hoped she hadn't upset Mom.

"Mom, maybe I shouldn't have said anything."

"No, Peggy, you were absolutely right to talk about this. Remember that your Dad and I want you to enjoy this skating experience. When the enjoyment leaves, then it's time to take a new look at what we're doing."

"But I don't want to quit skating."

"Then we don't want you to, either. Tell you what. Let's try this coach a little while longer. You've got to keep working for your Third test right now. Later, if the differences between you and your coach are still bothering you, we'll talk some more. If it's any help, remember there's something to be learned from everyone."

Soon Peggy signed up to enter the Southwest Pacific Competition for Juvenile Girls. Practicing hard, she realized she'd gained some strength since last year. She'd also grown a little taller and that seemed to make her layback spins and spirals look prettier because she was better proportioned. But the extension on her spiral wasn't too high yet, so her coach suggested some balletic stretching exercises to do at home. She found it really helped. Yes, just like Mom said, there was something to be learned from everyone.

Peggy added a double salchow to her program, practicing again and again the jump from a back inside edge on her left foot to a back outside edge on her right foot with two revolutions in the changeover. Now she was ready for the competition. This time, she wasn't quite as nervous, although she continued to feel shy before so many people. If only she could think of something that would keep her from worrying about the audience.

She easily won the Southwest Pacific championships held in December at the Iceland arena in Paramount. Then she sent in an application for the Pacific Coast event coming up in January.

"Where's the competition going to be held?" Janice asked one night at dinner.

"Some place called Squaw Valley," Peggy said.

"Where's that?" Maxine asked.

"It's in northern California," Dad told them. "Just a few miles from Lake Tahoe. More important, it's where the Olympic Games will be held in February."

"Is Peggy going to be in the Olympics?" Maxine asked. Her round eyes opened wide.

"No, but the Pacific Coast skaters will test the rink during their competition. If any problems come up, they can be smoothed out before the Games begin."

"Peggy can pretend she's in the Olympics now," Janice said. "And maybe, one day, she will be."

A month before the Olympics began, Peggy went to Squaw Valley. The countryside looked more spectacular than anything she'd ever seen. New snow lay on the ground and glinted in the bright sun. Towering Sierra peaks surrounded the compact little village. Everywhere she turned, pine trees were laden with snow that resembled mounds of whipped cream heaped on each branch.

As Mom pulled their car up before Blyth Memorial Arena, where the opening ceremonies would take place, Peggy was sure her heart leaped wildly into a double axel because of the feelings that overwhelmed her. How thrilling it was to have even so small a part in this event that would soon capture the attention of the sports world!

Peggy jumped out of the car and scooped some snow into her mouth and loved the cold, clean, fresh taste. Squaw Valley was an experience she would always remember.

Then the competition began and soon the compulsories were finished. Now Peggy looked forward to the free-style portion of the championships, the part she liked best.

Peggy never had skated outdoors in freezing weather like this before, nor on so large a rink before so many people. She sat wrapped in blankets until her turn came, then skated to the center of the ice and her music began. After she glided into her first spiral and felt the chilly air whipping her face, she forgot the weather and lost herself in the music and the rhythmic motion. She concentrated hard on every extension and spin and sometimes hardly felt the ice as she landed a jump. Oh, this feeling got better and better all the time. Stroking into her final double-toe spin, she timed it to the exact climax of the music. Then she dug her toe pick into the ice and stopped perfectly, focusing quickly on the flag pole so she wouldn't feel dizzy. After bowing, she skated off the ice, feeling her cheeks tingling in the freezing temperature. When everyone else had skated, the scores were announced and Peggy had won first place again.

Mom hurried up to her after she received her winner's cup and hugged her closely. Peggy looked over Mom's shoulder to see a slightly built man with wavy brown hair smiling at her.

"Hi." Peggy smiled at him.

"Peggy," Mom said. "This is Bill Kipp. He coaches at Iceland and came to Squaw Valley with several of his students who are competing, too."

Peggy liked Mr. Kipp's friendly manner. When they returned home after competition was finished, Mom arranged for Peggy to begin lessons with him. Under Mr. Kipp's guidance, Peggy soon passed the Fourth USFSA test and appeared as a solo skater in the Arctic Blades ice-skating revue. Now she really felt at home again, as she had with Mr. Turner.

One day, Mr. Kipp called her aside after class.

"Peggy, you've made yourself eligible for the Novice class by passing your Fourth test, and I think you're more than ready to move up, don't you?"

She didn't hesitate for more than a second. Peggy felt prepared to take a giant step forward. At her next patch session, she began to concentrate harder on her school figures. During lessons, she worked on a free-style program with Mr. Kipp.

Peggy also began to think about style now and what she wanted to look like on the ice. As she watched Mr. Kipp coach other skaters, some of whom had competed in the Olympics, she tried to decide what made each of them outstanding. Some were athletic, others were more dancer than skater. Others had a certain flair and used their bodies to express a movement or figure that was uniquely their own. Whatever it was, the skaters who had achieved this special class standing also displayed an individuality that was more than just knowing the figures. Although she was only twelve, Peggy realized it was important to begin developing her own style soon. Now, when Peggy wasn't skating, she was watching Mr. Kipp's champions: watching and learning and, sometimes, wondering— wondering if she'd ever be as good as they were.

Peggy was so prepared for the Southwest Pacific championships for Novice Girls that fall, she took first place and immediately moved on to the Pacific Coast competition in December. She felt at ease and confident until she entered the Polar Palace in Hollywood and saw the crowd. Peggy realized the free-style event was always well attended, but never had the realization become so personal. How would she get through the night if she thought about all those people sitting out there looking at her? She wished sometimes that the arrangement could be like her front porch, that the audience could see, yet not be seen by her.

Peggy slipped on her tights and skates, left foot first as usual, then put on a red skating dress and gave her short dark hair a final pat. She walked slowly to the rink and waited for the announcer to call her name. Standing in the shadows, she became aware of the people sitting in the front rows. What did they look like? If she could only imagine they were something else. Something that she wouldn't be frightened of. She closed her eyes tightly.

"Peggy," someone whispered in her ear.

"What?"

"What are you doing?" It was Joan, one of the girls who was competing tonight.

"I'm thinking."

"What about?"

Then Peggy had it. "Cabbages," she said, and giggled.

"Huh?" Joan said, and walked away. Peggy looked after her, knowing she must be puzzled, yet how could she explain? She just couldn't tell anyone about the cabbages sitting in the front row.

Her name was called and she skated with firm, strong strokes, trying to interpret the music in a way that she felt deep inside. Before she knew it, her three-minute free-style program was over and she warmed to the generous applause coming from the audience. No, she thought. The cabbages.

Later, when everyone had skated, the scores for school figures and free style were announced and Peggy had won first place in the Pacific Coast championship, Novice division. Mr. Kipp hurried up to her, even before her family reached her.

"Congratulations, Peggy. You can move up in competition again. We'll plan for it as soon as I come back."

"Where are you going, Mr. Kipp?"

"To coach our skaters from Paramount in the National championships at Colorado Springs, and then I'm traveling to Europe with the World's team."

Peggy couldn't believe it! Nationals! Then to Europe!

How she wished she could go, too. Not now, of course, she wasn't ready yet. But maybe soon, her time would come.

"Good luck, Mr. Kipp. I'll practice hard while you're gone."

"Good-bye, Peggy. I'll send you a postcard from Czechoslovakia."

But the postcard never came.

Maxine, Peggy and Janice Fleming try out their new roller skates. Peggy was six years old.

Nine-year-old Peggy is the cowgirl in this 1957 Halloween picture. She's shown with her sisters on the left, and Pat and Mike Nye on the right.

(above) Peggy Fleming, center, winner of the 1961 Pacific Coast championships, Novice Ladies division. (left) Peggy in 1962, when she was fourteen.

*(left) Peggy, aged fifteen, with
one of her first trophies.
(right) Peggy in 1963.*

Peggy modeling Olympic
clothes (1964).

In 1965 Peggy won 3rd
place in World's
competition in Colorado
Springs.

Peggy with coach Bob Paul and (right) when she was seventeen.

Peggy Fleming, after winning the 1966 ladies' senior Nationals title. Scott Ethan Allen, the mens' senior champion is on the left, and Ron and Cynthia Kauffman, pairs champions, are on the right.

(below) In the 1966 World competition, Peggy (center) won first place; Gabrielle Seyfert (right) of East Germany won second place; and Petra Burka (left) of Canada won third place.

5

Nationals, at Last!

When Peggy hurried home from school on an afternoon in mid-February, she thought the air felt heavy, as if it might rain soon. She hoped it would wait until she'd returned from her patch session at the Wintergarten tonight. Walking home in a downpour would be a good way to catch cold.

"I'm home," she called, as she entered the front door. She was startled to see Mom sitting in a darkened corner of the living room. Her eyes looked red, and her face was puffy as if she'd been crying.

"Peggy," she began. "I have some sad news to tell you."

"What is it? What's happened?"

"There's been an airplane accident." Mom hesitated for a moment.

"But who . . . "

"The United States figure-skating team, every single one of them, has been killed."

Peggy sat down heavily, stunned and unable, or perhaps unwilling, to understand what Mom had just said.

"Do you mean the kids from Paramount going to Europe?" Then slowly, ever so slowly, Peggy added, "Do you mean Mr. Kipp?"

"Yes, Peggy. Mr. Kipp was killed, too."

Later, Peggy turned on the television and heard the broadcast that told how all eighteen members of the United States Figure Skating team, on its way to the World's competition in Prague, Czechoslovakia, had been killed in a plane crash in Belgium. It would take years, the commentator said, to rebuild the team.

Peggy forced herself to go to the Wintergarten and follow through with her patch session, even though she started to cry whenever she thought of Mr. Kipp. There was no laughter in the arena today and no talking, just the grind, grind, grind of skate meeting ice as students grimly traced their figures. Then, as slowly and silently as they'd come in they left the arena, and when Peggy went home at dusk, she felt a light drizzle on her cheeks to mingle with the tears.

Doriann Swett, who was blonde and fragile-looking, became Peggy's new coach. Under her direction, Peggy began to prepare for competition at the next level, Junior Ladies. Slowly, over the months, Peggy learned to love her new teacher. She provided stability in Peggy's skating life after the death of Mr. Kipp and inspired her in striving for a more balletic style.

Peggy easily passed the Fifth USFSA test and continued to blossom under Miss Swett's remarkable teaching ability. The geometric-like figures that Peggy traced again and again on the ice were becoming increasingly complicated, but Peggy delighted in the challenge. Someone told her one day that she had a good head for figures. Secretly she wished her math figures at school came as easily to her as the compulsory school figures on ice.

In December Peggy competed in the Southwest regional championships at Iceland in Paramount and won in the Junior Ladies division. It was difficult to go to this competition for the first time after the tragedy, knowing she wouldn't hear Mr. Kipp's familiar voice or see the champions she'd watched so carefully.

A few weeks later, Peggy and Mom drove to Great Falls, Montana, for the Pacific Coast sectional meet, leaving Grandma Deal, Mom's mother, at home to run the house. Peggy thought she'd feel the cold weather here, maybe even more than at Squaw Valley. But she didn't. A strange weather pattern had arrived, bringing with it a hot, dry wind. She felt tired and her throat itched when she swallowed.

Stop worrying, Peggy told herself. That hot, dry wind is making your throat raspy. You're thirteen years old now, so don't be a baby about it. She continued to skate, hoping Mom and Miss Swett wouldn't notice anything was wrong.

Peggy took her regular practice time on the ice and then sat down in one of the rinkside seats to rest. It must be the altitude, she thought. Yes, that's it. She'd heard that skaters needed altitude conditioning and she didn't get much in Pasadena. Or maybe it was something else. Maybe it was the growing awareness of the importance of this competition that made her feel like she was wearing her skates on the wrong feet.

Miss Swett sat down beside her. "Everything okay?" she said in her own way.

"Oh, yes, fine." Peggy tried to sound like it.

"I suppose you're feeling the pressure as much as anything."

"I'm trying not to think about it."

"I wonder if that's wise, Peggy," Miss Swett said. "Sometimes it's better to talk things out. Problems don't seem so big once you've voiced your feelings about them."

Peggy thought a moment. She knew, if she finished in one of the top three positions tonight, she'd move up to the Nationals! Nationals, at last! She'd dreamed of nothing else while watching Mr. Kipp's kids at Paramount. But it was scary, serious business. A lump the size of an orange grew in her throat and refused to budge, even when she swallowed several times.

Miss Swett must have reading her mind. "You're ready for the Nationals, Peggy. Your figures are excellent. It's getting so no one can match you for technique, and I see the beginnings of a special quality to your free style that's unlike anyone else's."

"But . . . the other things, Miss Swett. I'll be up against kids from all over the country. Kids who've been skating lots longer than I have and have had more private lessons. And they have those expensive boots I've read about in magazines and fancy costumes from a special store instead of homemade ones and the girls have their hair set in beauty shops and . . . well, I just can't afford them." There, she'd said it all and now she was breathless with the wonder of having revealed those feelings.

"You will need better boots, soon, Peggy, but they needn't be the most expensive ones. In the meantime, remember that you've already got the best equipment that money can't buy."

Peggy turned a puzzled look at her coach. "What's that?"

"You and your own two legs."

"I guess I never thought of it that way."

"Lots of kids would love to skate as well as you do, Peggy. They don't have the talent, so they surround themselves with frills and feathers to hide what's missing in their performance. Make the most of what you've been given and compete only in the area where it really matters. Then the pressures at the higher level of competition won't be so difficult."

I hope so, Peggy thought. I hope so.

She awoke the next morning to skate her school figures, hoping the wobbles she felt inside didn't show up on the ice. Watching the judges, bundled up in overcoats and boots, as they contemplated her figures, Peggy began to feel light-headed. She couldn't see what they were looking at now. Was it a change loop or bracket they seemed to be so interested in? Suddenly, she couldn't remember what she'd skated. Her head felt as if she'd been doing a double toe spin all day. I'll feel better after

I've had a nap, Peggy thought. It was her custom to rest before an evening competition.

She went to the motel with Mom. "Are you sure it's only the weather that's bothering you?" Mom asked.

"I'm sure," Peggy said. But she didn't feel sure inside. Peggy stayed in bed until it was nearly time for the evening's competition. When she got up, Mom found she had a temperature.

"Peggy, I think you've got more than a reaction to the dry wind," she said, concern written on her features. "I'll go talk to the skating officials and see about cancelling your program."

"No, Mom, please." Her voice sounded like a rusty skate blade grinding over rough ice. "I can get through my program. After all, it's only three and a half minutes long. Then I'll come right back to bed, I promise."

Mom looked at her, "Peggy, I know how much you want to skate, but . . . "

"Then please let me."

Reluctantly, Mom gave her permission. Peggy dressed, combed her hair, noted her fiery cheeks and knew she didn't need any cosmetics tonight.

They reached the rink and she waited in the dressing room. If the other girls talked to her, she didn't notice. Then Mom came in.

"You're next, Peggy."

She rose and walked to the rink. Why was she doing this? Why did it matter so much? Was she trying to prove something to herself and the other kids? That she could skate despite obstacles because that's what champions are made of? Or was it because she wanted to be part of the

National figure-skating team that was slowly being rebuilt and she wanted to be noticed and considered?

Her music began and she stroked off, but her first jump told her what the performance would be like. Weak, wobbly and flat. She could barely sustain a spiral and the double salchow coming up in the program could only spell disaster. She tried. She tried hard but this had been a serious mistake and she knew it. She simply couldn't continue.

Abruptly she skated off the ice, noticing the rising murmur of voices coming from the spectators. Mom hurried up and threw her arms protectively around her, leading her away from the people who came forward to question and comment.

"That was the most courageous thing you've ever done, Peggy," she said, softly.

"And the hardest, Mom." Tears took over and cooled her burning face.

The next few days were blurred by illness. Peggy was too sick to be involved in the controversy that swirled about her incomplete performance. After a special meeting, the Pacific Coast committee gave her a letter to compete at the National Novice level based on her excellent school figures and previous record. Peggy felt grateful for their understanding and generosity.

At home, a week later, Peggy was still piecing her thoughts together. She wondered why she'd insisted on skating when she'd been so sick. Nothing had been proved except how little she knew about herself and her limitations. Perhaps she'd learned a valuable lesson, one better learned now rather than later. One thing she knew for certain. She'd been given a second chance and would do her best to make the most of it. Sighing, she gathered her school books together and prepared to catch up on homework. There was an awful lot to learn about competing that had nothing to do with skating, she thought.

In January, Peggy, accompanied by Mom, flew to Boston for the Nationals. During compulsories, Peggy's figures were precise and she grew increasingly excited about her chances. She looked forward to the second half of the competition.

On free-style night, Peggy hurried to the dressing room and put on her tights, then her skating dress of royal blue jersey with the glittery beads all over it. Mom really worked hard on this costume. Peggy knew she wanted it to be special for her first Nationals competition. Finally, she laced on her skates.

Peggy's name was announced and she skated to the center of the rink, trying not to bite her lips, a mannerism that would display the nervousness she felt. Remember the cabbages, she told herself.

Her music began and she stroked off, firm and hard, and she knew her program would have no flaws tonight. Her double lutz jump seemed airy and light and the audience liked it, judging from the applause. In the slow portion, she used arm movements that she had choreographed into the program after seeing a ballet recital. That had been so helpful and she wished she could see more ballet performances, but it was a rare occasion when she could find time for it.

The music seemed to lift her out of herself and she hardly felt the ice as she glided over it. The double axel near the end of the program felt properly placed and she whirled into a double toe spin that made her giddy with happiness as she bowed to the audience and skated off.

Peggy placed second. It was hard to accept at first, because she hadn't been beaten since the second time she'd competed. And that was the only time. Gradually, however, as she thought about it, Peggy realized it wasn't a defeat at all, it was a challenge. She flew home to California, determined to make the most of it.

6

An Important Decision

Peggy increased her practice time on the ice now, slipping out of bed at five-thirty in the morning, eating a hasty breakfast, then hurrying to the Wintergarten alone. The owner had given her a key to the side door, but she had to walk all the way to the center of the cavernous black arena to reach the light switch.

"Whew," she breathed when the lights turned the rink into an inviting place again.

Her friend, Susan, came a little while later and they shared the huge ice space, although they could use only the center to any advantage. The perimeter of the rink was always rough from the previous night's public session.

One morning, Peggy was a little late leaving home and met Dad at the back door, just returning from work. His job as pressman for the *Star News* demanded unusual hours.

"Wait, Peggy," he said. "I'll walk to the rink with you."

They hurried in the side door, turned on the lights and Peggy skated to the center of the rink. Susan soon joined her and Dad saw the problem almost immediately.

"The Wintergarten people are very generous to allow you girls use of the ice free-of-charge every morning," he said. "But we can't expect them to send a man down to clean it for you, too." Dad looked around and spotted the ice machine. "Unless, of course, that man is me." Looking at his blue eyes was like holding a mirror to her own, Peggy thought.

He walked to the ice machine that had always looked like a giant creeping, ice-chewing bug to Peggy and began to check it out. Peggy could hear Dad whistling and talking to himself and she knew he was analyzing just how to drive the motor and make the ice.

That afternoon, when Peggy returned from school, Dad said, "It's all settled, honey. The Wintergarten gave me permission to use the ice machine and tomorrow morning you'll have a rink that's smooth as glass to skate on."

They settled into a routine. Peggy had breakfast ready for Dad when he returned from work, then they hurried to the rink together. Peggy knew this extra chore for Dad was costing him precious sleep time. His part-time job in the afternoon to help pay for her skating lessons and ice time had already cut down on his chances for rest then. It worried her to see Dad work so hard, but when she tried to talk about it, he'd stop her with a hug and a kiss.

"Peggy, I can't explain it. Just remember always, what an unbelievable joy it is for me to do this. Maybe, someday, when you're a parent, you'll understand."

Peggy burrowed her head on Dad's shoulder, feeling the roughness of his sweater tickle her face and sniffing the outdoorsy scent of his soap. Yes, she hoped that someday she would understand Dad's feelings. Somehow, it seemed even better than winning.

As Peggy prepared for the Southwest Pacific and Pacific Coast competitions in November and December, she spent more and more of her time on the ice. She began to bring her schoolbooks with her, often propping them up on the railing around the rink. As she skated, she thought about what she'd just read in a history or English book. Occasionally, if she forgot, she slipped back to the railing for another glance at her lesson.

After winning first place in Southwest Pacific and Pacific Coast, Peggy looked forward to Nationals again being held in Long Beach in January. She would compete in the Junior division. At the age of fourteen and a half, Peggy felt ready to handle almost anything the competition had to offer.

Mom and Peggy drove down from Pasadena early in the morning on the first day of Nationals. Peggy took her practice time on the ice, then headed back to the dressing room to change. The door was slightly ajar as she approached and she heard voices coming from inside. One of them was talking about her!

"Can you believe that Peggy Fleming?" the voice said. "Did you see her practice those weird arm movements?"

"Yeah," the other voice agreed. "If she wants to be a ballerina, she ought to turn in her skates and get up on her tippy toes." Someone giggled.

Peggy felt her face flush with anger and she knew she shouldn't listen to another word. But she felt as if she'd taken root.

"Well, she won't go much further," the first voice said. "She isn't too strong, you know. She can hardly get off the ice on her axels."

Peggy ran blindly down the hall. She felt as if she'd just been run over by the ice machine. Hurrying outside the arena, she paced up and down, trying to get rid of the hostile feelings that threatened to overwhelm her. She knew she couldn't afford to let anything bother her now, perhaps ruin her concentration on the ice. Still, what if her balletic movements were too difficult? Did they look foolish? Now uneasiness followed, and she wondered if those girls could possibly be right.

Mom found her a little while later. "Peggy, come inside. You're going to wear yourself out."

Peggy tried to rest, but she just couldn't relax and her free-style program showed it. The usual feelings she displayed about her music was lacking. The flow from one figure to another seemed strained. It hadn't been a good performance and Peggy felt she got what she deserved: third place in National Juniors.

The rest of the family had driven down to see Peggy skate. Now they reflected her somber feelings as they drove home to Pasadena later that evening.

After Peggy slipped into bed and the lights were snapped off in the room she shared with Janice and Maxine, something soft and fluffy whizzed past her face. Giggling, she grabbed her pillow and threw it toward Janice's bed. Maxine turned on the lights and ducked as a pillow just missed her. Cathy ran in from her room, screaming like an overheated teakettle and threw her pillow at Janice. Peggy stood on her bed, and took accurate aim at Maxine.

"Gotcha!" she shouted, bouncing up and down.

The fight lasted no more than a couple of minutes, but at the end of it, the room had been demolished and so had Peggy's tense mood. As she lay under a pile of pillows, laughing so hard the tears ran down her cheeks, she knew why her sisters had started the pillow fight and loved them more than ever.

That night, lying quietly in bed, she resolved never, ever, to listen to gossip again. She personally vowed never to resort to this sort of locker-room technique to hurt someone else. It was mean and vicious and had no place in her plans.

"From now on," she whispered, as if taking a solemn vow, "I compete against no one else but me. I will work only to make my own skating better, not to beat someone else."

A few days later, Mom and Dad called a family conference.

"Peggy's performance at Nationals last week was not indicative of her ability," Dad began.

"What's that big word mean?" Cathy asked.

"She shoulda been first," Maxine said.

"Hooray for Peggy!" Cathy started the chant she usually reserved for Peggy's competitions.

"Cathy, come sit by me," Mom coaxed quietly.

Dad waited for his peppy eight-year-old to settle down, then continued. "What we need to decide is, what does Peggy do now? She is qualified to move up to National Senior Ladies next year, if she wants to."

Everyone looked around expectantly.

"The reason I'm asking everyone for an opinion is this," Dad said. "If Peggy decides to take the giant leap to Seniors, it means everyone will contribute, as well."

"Contribute what, Dad?" Maxine asked.

"I'll be working longer hours. Mom will be sewing and driving Peggy to extra lessons. And you girls will have to do your share of the chores around the house without being told. You'll have to help cook and clean and be responsible for one another."

Everyone seemed lost in thought for a few moments. Then Janice broke the silence.

"Dad," Janice cleared her throat. "If Peggy wins National Senior Ladies, does that mean she's champion of the whole United States?"

"Sure does, Janice," Dad said.

"Wow," Cathy breathed.

"We know Peggy's the best," Janice began. "I think it's time we let the rest of the country find that out, too."

"I vote with Janice," Maxine said.

"Me, too!" Cathy shouted, bouncing up and down on her chair.

"It's the only way to go, Al," Mom said softly.

"It's settled then," Dad said. They all looked at Peggy and smiled.

Peggy took a few weeks' vacation from the ice during the early spring. At last she had time to catch up on schoolwork as well as begin some sewing projects with her sisters. Janice, Peggy and Maxine had learned the basics of sewing in junior high. Now, with Mom's expert guidance, they turned out most of their own school clothes. Peggy loved to go with her sisters and browse through fabric shops. With Maxine and Janice offering advice, Peggy often came home with many ideas for future skating costumes.

Then it was summer and her freshman year in high school came to a close. Peggy was delighted to have extra time to devote to the ice. Because she wanted to add more balletic feeling to her programs, she began to study with Bob Turk, a former champion, who now specialized in choreography.

In addition to these activities, Peggy and Mom drove to the public library several times a week to listen to music. They put on headsets and played one record after another in hopes of finding just the right skating music for next winter's Nationals competition.

One day Peggy put down her headset and walked to the drinking fountain. A boy, loaded down with books, stepped out of the stacks and headed her way. Suddenly Peggy recognized him. It was Jeff, who had sat in front of her in English class last semester. She remembered that he combed his curly brown hair all the time.

"Hi, Peggy," he said, his dark eyes sparkling with

recognition. "What are you doing here? I mean, I thought you'd be skating."

"You've got the wrong idea about me, Jeff. I don't skate every minute of my life."

"Hey, you mean it? I mean, do you have time to do other things, like go to a movie if someone asked you, or play tennis or go bicycle riding?"

"Sure, of course I do." Peggy wondered if all the kids at school thought she was some kind of skating machine. Well, maybe her life seemed a little unusual, even weird, to them, but did that mean she wasn't interested in the same things as her friends? Things like boys and dates?

Jeff grinned, displaying his braces. "I'll call you real soon. See you, Peg." He walked down the hall as Peggy looked after him. Maybe she'd finally have a real live date before the summer was over.

7

Back to Cleveland

$\mathcal{A}$lthough Peggy had time for friends and family that summer, she never missed a lesson with her new coach, Peter Betz. He emphasized stretching exercises for a better line as well as hard work on figures to pass the Eighth and final USFSA test.

Her sisters occasionally came with her when Peggy went to the rink for practice sessions. Maxine stroked slowly and steadily around the ice, but Cathy zipped past everyone. Lessons had given Cathy confidence to try spins and jumps and she was showing talent, Peggy observed.

Peggy enjoyed her sisters' company on the ice and off. At home they continued to sew together or to watch

Janice as she took over the kitchen and practiced a new recipe. They still shared household duties, too, with lists of chores drawn up each week for them to do. No one liked to work outdoors except Maxine, so she was the one who kept the grass mowed.

Perhaps one of the favorite times for all the family was when Dad decided to cook his special spaghetti. Then everyone, even Janice, stayed out of the kitchen and waited in anticipation for dinner.

That summer she turned fifteen and it seemed great in one special way for Peggy. It was special because she found time to relax and enjoy friends like Linda and Susan at slumber parties and tennis games and movie dates with boys like Jeff. She was sorry to see it end when school began in September.

Slowly the tempo increased in her training program now, as she built toward Nationals in January. Sometimes she had difficulty finding ice time and she skated an hour at this rink, then an hour at another. It wasn't helping her concentration and she worried about it.

From mid-November on, she prepared for the big step to National Senior ladies and maybe . . . just maybe . . . qualifying for the Olympics in February. She was up at five-thirty every morning, practiced on the ice until eight-thirty, when it was time for school, back to the rink by three-thirty and more practice until five. Then home for a brief rest and dinner and back to the ice for another hour or two.

Now everything feels right about Nationals, Peggy thought one day as she ended a patch session. She was ready mentally and physically. In fact, ever since she'd learned that Nationals would be held in Cleveland in the rink where she began skating with Mrs. Lapish, Peggy felt it was a good omen. Not even hearing that some of the officials had ranked her eleventh out of eleven competitors for this event dampened her feelings of something wonderful about to happen.

Finally, the day came and it was time to go. Peggy snapped her packed suitcase shut, then lifted it off the bed and put it on the floor beside her skate bag. She looked around the bedroom once more, to see if she'd forgotten anything for the trip to Cleveland and to make sure everything looked neat. She closed her dresser drawers, then scooped up a pair of socks lying by the bed and put them in the clothes hamper. After straightening the bedspread, she felt satisfied. Now she could leave.

She carried the suitcase and bag into the living room and put them down beside the low cedar chest on which all of her skating trophies were displayed. Looking at them now, as if she'd never seen them before, Peggy wondered if she would bring home one more to join these or if . . . but she wouldn't think of defeat. She'd only think of doing her best.

Her sisters came in from the kitchen, where they'd just finished breakfast. Cathy carried a piece of toast. "How far do you think Mom and Dad have driven?"

"Let's see." Peggy counted on her fingers. "They started four days ago. They're probably in Ohio by now. Anyway, I know they'll meet my plane when I get to Cleveland late this afternoon."

Janice said, "I wish Mom and Dad could have gone on the plane, too. Seems like a long way to drive, especially this time of year in the Midwest."

"I know," Peggy said. "But Dad said it cost too much for all of us to fly."

"Why are you flying, then?" Cathy's questions were always as direct as the look from her round blue eyes.

"Because I can't stay off the ice four straight days before a competition," Peggy explained patiently. She wondered, sometimes, if her sisters resented the attention and money being spent on her skating career. It would be natural for them to feel that way, she supposed, and she couldn't really blame them.

There was the sound of automobile brakes.

Maxine looked out the window overlooking the front porch. "Dad's friend, Mr. Balser, just drove up, Peggy."

They rushed to her and she kissed each one, giving Cathy a fierce hug.

"I wish I could go, too." Cathy's bright face clouded over.

"So do I, oh, so do I."

"Good luck, Peg," Janice said.

"Yeah, Peg," Maxine echoed.

Mr. Balser knocked on the door and Peggy picked up her suitcase and skate bag. "Bye," she said and hurried out to the car before she started to cry.

As they headed for the freeway, Peggy said, "Thank you, Mr. Balser, for driving me to the airport."

"Glad to do it, Peggy. Your dad's helped me out at work many a time, so I'm happy to return the favor now." He launched into a story to emphasize the point. As Peggy listened, she looked at the kids walking to high school a short distance away. If she weren't entered in competition now, she'd be walking along in the January sunshine with them, then going to class and, later, eating lunch with friends like Susan or Linda or Jeff. She missed them when she left like this for a couple of weeks, yet she knew she'd miss skating too, if she had to give that up. Sometimes she felt torn between her two worlds and wondered what it would feel like to live in just one.

Now, however, all her thoughts had to be centered on her world of skating. Cleveland and the competition there would be her only world for the next few days.

When she walked into the Cleveland ice arena the next morning, Peggy's immediate reaction was, "It's not nearly as large as I remembered."

As she warmed up before the school-figures competition began, Peggy looked around at the other skaters, the spectators and the judges, always bundled up as if they expected the Ice Age to return at any moment. Here and there she caught a glimpse of a face that looked familiar. Was that Karen, she wondered, way across the ice? And where was Mrs. Lapish? She didn't see her now, but after the figures, she hoped to find her.

Order came as the announcer asked that the rink be cleared and competition begin. The draw to decide which figures would be skated and which foot to skate them on already had taken place. Peggy was pleased with the results. She sat down, wrapped in a blanket, and waited her turn.

The days passed quickly, and at the end of compulsories, Peggy occupied third place, behind Lorraine Hanlon of Boston and Christine Haigler of Colorado Springs. Lorraine and Christine are such terrific skaters, Peggy thought. And so is Tina Noyes from Boston, right behind me, in fourth. I'll really have to skate my best tomorrow in free style, to stay in third and qualify for the Olympics.

There was no one in the old familiar dressing room the next evening when she entered. She sighed gratefully. More and more, she liked to be alone for a little while before competition. Slowly Peggy dressed, first inspecting her boots carefully for spots and her tights for runs or tears. As she put them on, left foot first, she suddenly realized it was a habit she'd established over the years. No sense in breaking the string now, she thought, pulling her blue matte jersey dress over her head. Then she looked at herself in the mirror.

Would she ever stop looking like a toothpick, she wondered. Probably five foot three was as tall as she'd get, but surely she'd start to curve in and out sometime. And those freckles! No matter what she did to conceal them, they were always poking through. She brushed her short dark hair till her scalp tingled, powdered over her freckles and decided she was ready.

Other contestants drifted in now, and although she smiled and said hello, she retreated to her own quiet spot deep inside her. Then it was time. Someone said, "Peggy, you're next."

She skated to the center of the ice, feeling the warmth of the spotlight on her. Although she knew there were thousands of people watching, she felt alone with her music as it began. *The Art of the Prima Ballerina* opened slowly and she matched its graceful, majestic strains with movements that were soft and fluid, yet in firm control. Her first double axel came early in the program and seemed surprisingly easy, but she didn't relax. She didn't let down for a second. One of her coaches once said letting down after a good figure separated the champions from the runners-up.

Staying right with the music, she let the violins guide her as she used the balletic arm positions she'd carefully choreographed into this section. Now the delayed axel. She felt briefly suspended in midair for a magic moment, before landing perfectly on that back outside edge. Her elevations were fantastic tonight and her spirits soared to match them.

Now she whirled into a layback spin which she was beginning to think of as her trademark because she could bend back so far. As the music increased in tempo, so did her self-assurance, although she was beginning to tire slightly now. She stroked into a final spin knowing she'd skated like a champion tonight. Oh, what a great feeling! The swell of the applause, even before she finished, confirmed it. When she stopped, tears of joy rolled down her cheeks. She bowed several times, but the audience wouldn't stop applauding!

Finally she skated off and there were Mom and Dad, laughing and crying and hugging her all at once.

Later, after everyone had performed, the winners were announced. Christine Haigler skated out to receive her third-place prize and Tina Noyes followed to receive second. Then the announcer said, "The new National Senior Ladies champion, from Pasadena, California, Miss Peggy Fleming."

She felt surprised and scared and happy and numb all at the same time when she skated out to accept her trophy. It was a miracle that she could make it to the winner's platform at all. The tears started again, although she tried to control them as she waved to the approving audience. Several photographers were taking pictures now and she didn't want to look like a crybaby.

"Congratulations, Peggy," Tina whispered.

"Olympics, here we come," Christine whispered on the other side of her.

The Olympics! That was the unbelievable part. She was now a member of the Olympic team that would represent the United States next month in Austria.

Finally the photographers were finished and Peggy, Tina and Christine were allowed to leave. As they came off the ice, a reporter hurried up to Peggy. She wanted to run away from him, but knew she had to conquer her shyness somehow. She swallowed hard and tried to think of her cabbages.

"How does it feel, at fifteen and a half, to be the youngest girl in skating history to win the National Senior Ladies championship?"

"It's about the best feeling in the whole world," Peggy managed to say.

"What goal do you have for the Olympics next month?" The reporter followed her as she headed for the dressing room.

Goal, she thought. How can you put in words all the

feelings and dreams and wishes that make a goal? Finally, she said, "Just represent my country the best I know how. By skating as well as I can."

She wondered, as she closed her door of the dressing room, if her best would be good enough for her first international competition.

8

Olympics, 1964

The next days were blurred with activity. Dad returned to California while Peggy and Mom flew to New York for a hectic week. There, one appointment followed after another. Peggy was fitted with new boots and all her Olympic clothes. Newspaper and television reporters interviewed her. She went shopping with Mom at Macy's for material that would be sewn into new skating dresses.

In the midst of this, Peggy slipped away to a rink alone and tried to put in some practice time, but she was immediately recognized and that was the end of her patch session. Mothers brought their children up to Peggy for autographs and advice and she tried to accommodate them all. She remembered how much a smile or word from Mr. Kipp's champions had meant to her.

But after Peggy skated off the ice she became increasingly concerned. How can I stay in condition at this rate, she wondered. Then, as she was preparing to leave, a small, well-dressed woman, about her mother's age, approached her.

"Hello," she said. "I'm Mrs. Kennedy, a member of the skating club here. I think you can use a place to practice where you won't be interrupted."

"Oh, can I ever," Peggy said.

"I'd like to invite you and your mother to stay at my home on Long Island." She smiled pleasantly at Peggy. "There's a small rink nearby which you can use privately until you fly to Europe."

Peggy just stared at Mrs. Kennedy unbelievingly. "Do you really mean it? Gosh, Mrs. Kennedy, no one's ever done anything for me like this before. I mean, it's just great. How can I ever thank you?"

Mom shared her delight. "Thank you so much," Mom said.

After Peggy and Mom moved to Mrs. Kennedy's home, she resumed her normal training routine immediately and kept to its strict schedule until they boarded the plane for Innsbruck, Austria, where the Olympics would open on January 29.

Peggy was so exhausted from the last few weeks' activities that even her first trip to Europe couldn't keep her awake and she slept through much of the flight. When they arrived at Innsbruck, however, she felt rested and eager to see this part of the world.

As the bus drove down Maria-Theresien-Strasse, Innsbruck's main street, Peggy wasn't prepared for its picture-postcard beauty. Snow lay everywhere, dapplying the gabled, red-roofed houses and turreted buildings. Looking closely into the brightly lighted stores, Peggy saw luscious displays in sausage and pastry shop windows.

The kids in the seat behind her must have been looking at the same shops.

"Dig those crazy hot dogs," a young man's voice said. "And look at those cream puffs with that curly whipped cream on top. And those pies . . . "

"Stop it," a girl's voice interrupted. "I'm on a diet and you're driving me out of my mind."

Other voices joined in now. "Look at that big statue in the middle of the street. Who is it? Some queen?"

"No, it's the Virgin Mary."

"Hey, look at the mountains up ahead. They look like a wall of pure rock facing the town."

"I'm glad I'm not a skier."

Peggy's eyes darted first one way, then another, trying to imprint the entire scene in her mind. But it was hopeless. She was so excited that nothing registered more than fleetingly at the moment. Maybe later, she could walk down the main street and quietly enjoy its beauty.

Soon she was settled into a room in Olympic Village with Tina and Christine. Mom stayed at a small hotel nearby. On opening day, Peggy participated with twelve hundred other athletes in gay and colorful ceremonies under bright blue skies. Peggy marched with the others in their Olympic uniforms, listened to the music and speeches and looked at the flags of every participating nation fluttering in the light breeze. Then she decided she was the luckiest girl in the world. Now, she thought. I'm here. I'm really here.

Pair skating began that evening and Peggy watched closely. Although the Russian couple, Ludmilla Belausova and Oleg Protopopov, won and she admired their flawless precision, it was the West German couple in second place who captured Peggy's full attention. Marika Killius and Hans-Juergen Baumler were brilliant skaters who inter- preted their music emotionally within the discipline of precise figure-skating technique. Peggy realized her skat- ing was similar to theirs and knew she could learn much from watching them. Fantastic, she thought. Watching them gives me goose bumps the size of the Alps. I'm so excited, I won't be able to sleep a second tonight.

The following day, when Peggy got up to prepare for skating the first two school figures, she felt a raspiness in her throat that hadn't been there the night before. Oh, no, she thought. Not again.

"What's the matter, Peggy?" Tina asked. "You're not getting sick, are you?"

"I hope not," she answered. "But my throat sure feels funny."

"I heard there's flu going around." Christine shrugged into her parka. "You better take something for it before it really gets you down."

"Christine, you know she can't take any pills unless they're approved by the Olympics people," Tina said.

"Oh, gosh, that's right." Christine pulled on her gloves. "Then you better see the team doctor, Peggy. He'll know what to do."

"I'll go after compulsories," Peggy said, hoping she wasn't heading for a repeat of Great Falls.

Peggy skated the first figure and found herself in eleventh place. The position didn't upset her, however, since she realized international competition was as finely sharpened as a new pair of skate blades. She watched Sjouke Dijkstra of Holland, the world's champion, skate with confidence and precision. Later, she took a commanding lead with just two figures. Wow, Peggy thought. What control. Then Peggy skated her second figure and moved up to sixth place. Good, she thought. Everything's improving but my throat.

Peggy skipped the ping-pong games and dancing and the Abbott-and-Costello movies on television and went to bed right after dinner, only to sleep fitfully during the night. Next morning, she realized she didn't feel much better. Compulsories were finished that day and Peggy slipped to eighth place after she skated the loop. She placed it poorly and couldn't correct it in the tracing.

By free-style competition on Sunday, Peggy had overcome most of her sore throat, but the illness left her shaky and weak. She dressed carefully, then began her customary quiet wait in the dressing room as other contestants drifted in and out. Christine left to skate a strong, self-assured program. Tina, Peggy knew, planned to open her program with a double flip, a double axel and a double toe loop. And that was just for openers, Peggy thought.

And then it will be my turn, Peggy thought. Suddenly the thought reached out and grabbed her. Me, she said to herself. Skinny, little Peggy Gale Fleming from Pasadena. I'm skating in the Olympics! Pinch me, world, to make sure I'm awake and not dreaming this.

Someone announced her name and she skated to the center of the rink. Using the same music and program that had won Nationals for her, she emphasized the balletic qualities even more. But she was nervous before this crowd of eleven thousand and her attempt to visualize cabbages in the front rows didn't help much. And then it happened. What she'd had nightmares about, chewed her nails over. She fell down right in front of the whole world watching on television! Quickly she picked herself up and continued, nothing bruised but her peace of mind. Now she was tiring so rapidly, the end of the program couldn't come soon enough. She bowed and skated off, relieved that her performance was over.

When the points were counted, she finished sixth, Christine seventh and Tina eighth. Her free-style performance had been good enough to pull her up two places, but not to the bronze medal some sports writers had predicted.

The closing ceremonies of the Olympics on February 9 moved with pageantlike precision through one colorful step after another. First, fanfares introduced the shield carriers and flag bearers, then all of the competitors marched into the stadium once more. The Olympic flag was lowered and carried out by eight gold-medal winners. The Greek flag, the Austrian flag and finally the French flag were raised to snap in the breeze. Peggy knew the French flag indicated that the 1968 Winter Olympics would be held in Grenoble. I'll be there, she decided. I'll really have to work, but I want to do it more than anything in the world.

Finally, Mr. Avery Brundage, President of the International Olympic Committee, declared the ninth Winter Olympics over. Peggy sighed with regret. It had been the most exciting two weeks of her life.

She and Mom flew on to Dortmund, Germany, for her first World's competition on February 25. Peggy knew the World's was an international competition just as the Olympics was, except it was held annually and the Olympics every four years. Although she had fully recovered from the virus that caused her sore throat, Peggy felt a certain lack of self-assurance and physical confidence. It helped to watch the World's champions carefully, particularly Marika Killius, who skated with Hans Baumler. She's so beautiful and elegant, Peggy thought. How can I ever be like her?

As Peggy went through this competition, she began to realize two facets of her skating needed more concentration: stamina and school figures. Nearly every city she'd skated in had higher elevation than Pasadena and it was altitude skating that was draining her now, wearing her down and tiring her before she finished a program. And her school figures. They were good, even excellent most of the time, but she realized if she were to continue in international competition, her schools must be flawless.

Peggy finished seventh in the overall World's competition and felt somewhat discouraged as she returned to the hotel and packed to go home. She wasn't prepared for the letter Mom showed her when she walked into their room.

"Peggy, look what was in our box downstairs."

Peggy saw the letter had been sent by the International Skating Union. Quickly her eyes raced over the page, her heart beginning to race in time. The ISU wanted her to go on the World's Championships tour with them. Only thirty international top skaters were picked to go, she knew, and now she was asked to be one of them!

She and Mom hugged each other, laughing and crying at the same time. "They like me, they like me," Peggy shouted, dancing around the room. After she settled down, Peggy helped Mom write a letter home with the good news.

The next several weeks fragmented into scenes at airports, hotels and skating rinks in one city after another. Peggy skated two performances a night in cities throughout Italy, Switzerland, France and West Germany. When she wasn't skating, she sat at rinkside and admired as the World's team skated their exhibition programs, playing to the audience and enjoying a certain freedom they weren't able to bring to a competitive performance. Peggy studied the girls' costumes and hair and makeup carefully. They looked like finished champions.

After Peggy finished skating the exhibition one night in Oberstdorf, Germany, she attended a festive dinner party given for members of the World's team. There was rich, German food, merry music and much laughter. Later, she joined in the dancing. When it was time to return to the hotel, she and Mom rode a cable car up the side of a mountain where their hotel was situated. Peggy thought this was the most unusual place for a hotel that she'd ever seen. She'd never forget it. Now she was suddenly tired and could think of nothing but a hot bubble bath and bed.

"Here is your key, madame," the concierge said to Mom. "And this notice of an overseas telephone call. Someone from Pasadena, California, tried to reach you earlier this evening. He asked that you return the call immediately upon your arrival."

"Thank you," Mom said, taking the note.

They walked upstairs in silence. Peggy wondered what was going on at home that could have prompted the expensive telephone call. She glanced at Mom out of the corner of her eye, wanting to ask what she thought, but she found Mom's face troubled and withdrawn. She decided to say nothing.

Inside their room, Mom dialed and they waited. Overseas telephone calls seemed to take forever, especially this late at night. Finally, Peggy heard Mom begin talking to Uncle George, Dad's brother.

"Hello, George, how are you?" Then Mom listened as her face slowly lost all color and she gripped the edge of the bed for support. Her voice fell to a whisper. "We're coming on the next plane."

"What's the matter?" Peggy asked. She thought she'd suffocate with panic.

"Dad's sick." Mom forced the words from her mouth. "He's had a heart attack . . . a bad one. We've got to go home tonight."

Oh, no, Peggy thought. Not Dad. Dad can't die. He just can't.

"Let's hurry, Mom," she whispered. "Let's hurry."

9

New Challenges

No one was allowed to see Dad at the hospital but Mom, and then only for a few minutes at a time. The days and weeks dragged by, as if they were anchored to big lead weights, until one day Mom came home and told them the good news.

"Dad's being moved out of intensive care tomorrow," she said. "Janice and Peggy will be able to see him then."

"What about me?" Cathy said, tears welling in her eyes. "I want to see Daddy, too."

"Honey, the hospital has certain rules," Mom began.

Cathy didn't wait to hear more. She ran from the room and Maxine followed.

"This has been so hard on all of you," Mom said. "And

you've been so good." Her voice broke and for a few moments she cried all the tears she'd held back for so long.

Peggy was more nervous when she went to see Dad the following day than she had been during any competition. She wanted to be cheerful and tell Dad all about the Olympics, but she was afraid she'd break down and cry. And she knew Dad didn't need a big scene. He couldn't be upset, Mom said. Not at all.

She and Janice walked into the room together. "Hi, Dad," she managed. He turned toward them and Peggy thought she'd choke inside. He looked as pale as the pillow cover and it seemed he'd shrunk somehow. And worse. There was no sparkle in his eyes, just an echo of the pain he must have felt. He didn't look like Dad at all.

"Hi, Peggy. Janice." They looked at one another for a moment, then Janice reached over and kissed Dad. She seemed to know what to do. Peggy followed, hoping Dad wouldn't notice her silly quivery mouth.

"Janice, I want to tell you something." Dad's voice seemed to be coming from far away. "You were so wonderful the night I got sick. You kept your head and handled everything just right."

"Thanks, Dad."

"You're going to make a fine nurse one day. I know it."

"I hope you come home real soon, so I can practice on you."

"I'll be there the minute the doctor says I can leave."

"We better go, Dad," Peggy said. "We don't want to wear you out."

"We'll be back tomorrow."

That night Peggy had a heart-to-heart talk with Mom. "I'm going to quit skating," she blurted out.

"Why, Peggy?" Mom asked. "Don't you like to skate anymore?"

"Yes, but it's not fair to the rest of the family," Peggy said. "Skating is so expensive and now that Dad can't work for awhile . . ." She let the thought just hang there between them.

"Don't worry," Mom assured her. "We'll get along just fine. We have investments and some insurance that will carry us through."

"I still think I should quit," Peggy insisted.

"When Dad comes home, we'll talk about it again," Mom said.

There were many visits to the hospital before Dad finally was allowed to come home. Several days after he walked into the house with slow, hesitant steps, he said, "Time for a family conference."

They pulled up chairs in the living room and waited. "There's a rumor going around that you're thinking about quitting, Peggy," he said.

Peggy blinked. Of course Mom would have told Dad.

"Peggy, you can't quit," Maxine said, flinging her long hair back over her shoulders. "You just can't. You're the champion."

"Peggy, you can't quit, 'cause I won't let you." Cathy's voice rose dramatically and everyone laughed.

"Looks like we've got a difference of opinion," Dad said.

"What do you think I should do, Dad?" Peggy asked.

"Peggy, you know how I feel, but that isn't the

important issue. It's what you want to do that counts. Do you want to quit?"

"I just thought it would be better—well, easier—if I quit, that's all." She looked at their faces and realized she'd misjudged their support. They were behind her more than ever.

"You've been invited to skate in that exhibition at Sun Valley when school is out this summer," Mom reminded her. "Why don't you work on that program before you make a final decision?"

Peggy knew that once she began on this exhibition program, using "Ave Maria" for her music, she'd never turn back. This music inspired her in a way that music hadn't reached her before. Mom was pretty wise in getting her to lose herself in this program.

The pace of Dad's recovery was much quicker than they'd anticipated and he urged Mom to go with Peggy to Sun Valley. "I've got the world's three prettiest nurses," he said, smiling at Peggy's sisters.

In the midst of the Sun Valley exhibition, she and Mom met Bob Paul. He was a Canadian gold-medal pairs champion in the 1960 Olympics, now teaching and chore-ographing in California. Young and darkly handsome, he had a magnetic personality and an enthusiasm for skating that made young skaters follow him wherever he went. Peggy felt fortunate when he agreed to coach her.

Following the exhibition, she began to go to the Pickwick Arena in Burbank several times a week that summer and fall for lessons with Bob. First he tackled the problem of Peggy's stamina by having her pace the ice for certain periods each day. Sometimes he paced with her.

"Peggy," Bob said one day as they went round and round the rink. "What do you want to look like on the ice? I have to know before we begin your choreography because you must skate the way you look and feel."

Peggy thought a moment, as she had so many times, about this subject. But no one else had ever asked her about it before. Now, could she put all the thoughts, finally, into words?

"I want to look pretty," she said, slowly. "And I want to look like I love skating, because I do. But more, I want everyone else to enjoy what I'm doing. Whether they like athletics, or ballet, or music, I want the audience to enjoy my performance, because it will be a combination of all three."

"You've just told me what the Peggy Fleming look is," Bob said. "Now, let's put it all together."

A silent line of communication developed between Peggy and Bob. Whenever Peggy felt an interpretation or set of figures and jumps wasn't working, she never had to say so. Her sixth sense of knowing what was right or wrong for her soon telegraphed itself to Bob, and together they worked out a variation that suited Peggy's style. He sensed the moods she wanted to evoke on the ice better than anyone else ever had.

And there were a few times when Peggy went limp as a dishrag. "What happened, Peggy?" Bob would ask. "Leave your bones at home today?" Then she knew he understood the sudden case of nerves she'd developed about the coming Nationals or an exhibition, and they'd quit for awhile. But not for long. Bob believed in discipline and soon they were at work again. He skated right behind her as she went through the intricate routine, shouting directions and advice over the music.

"Get your hip down," he'd yell, as she moved into a spiral. "And your head up." Later, he shouted, "That was a klutz of a lutz. You can do better than that."

Peggy appreciated Bob's lessons because the discipline was interlaced with fun and she began to contribute her share. One day, watching closely for the right opportunity, she waited till a break, then hid his contact lenses. Putting on her best Little Miss Innocent act, she worked hard through the rest of the lesson, although it was all she could do to keep the laughter inside from bursting out. Whenever a giggle surfaced, she channeled it into a cough.

After the lesson, Bob skated to Peggy's side as she circled the ice to slowly cool off.

"Good session today, Peggy," he said.

"Thanks, Bob."

"By the way, what did you do with them?"

Peggy looked up, startled.

"My contacts," he said. "You were so good today, you just had to be guilty." Bob laughed, then Peggy joined in.

"I can never fool anyone for long," she said.

There was little time for a vacation before she began the final training program for the Nationals. Returning to the competition as the champion of the United States, Peggy knew the eyes of the country's skating world would be watching her and she wanted to be ready for the scrutiny. In early February, Peggy flew to Lake Placid, New York, for the competition. There she saw her skating friends from around the country, skating friends who also became her friendly competitors during the event. Christine Haigler got off to a shaky start because of an old back injury. Soon, however, she pulled ahead of Peggy during compulsories and eventually won that part of the competition. In fact, Peggy never had beaten Christine in school-figures competition and Peggy knew she'd have to work hard in free style to retain her title.

On February 13, Peggy gave a spectacular free-style performance and received marks as high as 5.9 from the judges. Since six was a perfect score, Peggy's spirits soared as high as her jumps when her marks were announced. She had won her second National Senior Ladies' title.

She and Mom flew to Colorado Springs for the World's competition to be held there at the Broadmoor Hotel skating arena. Peggy fell in love with the Broadmoor immediately. Giant evergreens presided over the hotel's gently rolling lawns. Its long patio faced a lagoon patrolled by fat, haughty ducks. Westward, the Rockies loomed against the sky.

Inside, the skating facilities were near perfection. The rink was huge, the dressing rooms spacious and comfortable. Everything had been designed for the skater's concentration and comfort.

When she and Mom called home one night, Peggy bubbled over with enthusiasm about the Broadmoor.

"It's so neat to skate there, Dad," Peggy said. "And you'd love Colorado, too."

Later, during the competition, Peggy tired while performing at Colorado Spring's altitude. She finished third in World's, which was a great improvement over last year, but she realized she needed additional training. Dad was already planning ahead when they returned to Pasadena.

"Next year's World competition is going to be held in Davos, Switzerland," Dad said when he came home from work one day. "Before then, you've got to get some altitude conditioning. Wouldn't it be great if it could be in Colorado Springs?"

He smiled at Mom and Peggy wondered what they had in mind.

10

Carlo and Colorado

*P*eggy, accompanied by Mom, soon left on an ISU tour of major cities of the United States. Their suitcases were always heavy with Peggy's schoolbooks and she studied hard between rehearsals and performances.

When they returned home a few weeks later, Peggy couldn't believe Dad's words. "How'd you like to train at the Broadmoor?" he greeted her and Mom as they stepped off the plane. "As much ice time as you want will be yours and your coach will be none other than Carlo Fassi."

Carlo Fassi! What a magic name to Peggy. She knew him by reputation as an Italian World's champion who had become one of this country's best coaches. Now he would be her coach, too!

"It's the answer to all my dreams, Dad," Peggy said, hugging him. Chills of anticipation about the move ran up and down her spine as she thought of the beautiful skating facilities offered at the hotel. She'd also become a member of the Broadmoor Skating Club, an organization with an outstanding reputation for producing members who skated at the National level. If Peggy weren't feeling the warm California sunshine on her face, she'd know she was dreaming for sure.

Peggy and her family moved to Colorado as soon as school was out. Almost immediately, before she could begin training with Carlo, it was time to tour Europe with the ISU.

"I'll see you in the fall," Carlo said. "Then we shall make your school figures perfect."

Peggy and Mom flew to Europe again and soon reached Davos, Switzerland. Peggy knew Davos from previous tours and was now beginning to think of it as her European home town. Most of the cities on tour looked alike after awhile, but Davos was special. Whether it was the people or the locale or the shops and food, or some special combination, Davos really reached out to her.

One night, after a performance, the stage manager handed Peggy a note. "This came for you earlier, Peggy."

A fan letter, she thought, as she tore it open. She didn't like them too much because they were usually so sticky and sweet, but she always read them because someone cared enough to write.

"Dear Peggy: I'm a student at Colorado College in Colorado Springs," the note began. "I also take lessons from Carlo. Since I'm touring Europe with two friends this summer, Carlo suggested I say hello to you. If there's anything I can do for you while you're in Davos, let me know. Sincerely, Greg Jenkins."

Peggy arranged to meet Greg and his friends after the exhibition performance the following night.

"I'm a premed student at CC," he told her, as they walked along the streets in the warm balmy evening. "This summer, I'm taking German here in Europe and having a look around at the same time."

Although Peggy was attracted to Greg, whose quiet good looks cloaked a warm sense of humor, she had no time to become interested in a boyfriend now. She couldn't allow her concentration to waver for an instant this coming year. Still, he looked like someone she would like to know better sometime.

They talked a little more about skating with Carlo and school and living in Colorado Springs. As they said good-bye that evening, Peggy wondered if she'd see him soon or ever again. Although they'd be living in the same town, she knew their busy schedules might not leave any time for socializing. And besides, she told herself firmly, you don't have the time anyway, so forget it. And she thought she did.

When Peggy returned to Colorado late in the summer of 1965, it was time to enroll in Cheyenne Mountain High School for her senior year. Maxine became a sophomore at the same school while Cathy enrolled at the junior high just a few blocks away. Janice fulfilled a lifelong ambition and began nurse's training at Penrose Hospital. The family moved into a new house not far from the Broadmoor and Dad began to work as a pressman for the local newspaper. A family friend, Sandy Sills, came to live with them. When she became Peggy's roommate, they plastered their bedroom walls with poster pictures of the Jefferson Airplane and other rock groups.

Dad immediately benefited from the clear Colorado air. Color returned to his cheeks; he gained some weight and best of all, Peggy thought, the familiar bright sparkle returned to his eyes. Together, they planned family outings that gave Dad the right kind of exercise he needed. They picnicked, hiked easy mountain trails and in the winter discovered snow sports. As a family they'd never been happier.

When Greg discovered Peggy was living nearby, he began to call. Peggy decided that life could never be more perfect, not even if she lived to be one hundred.

And Carlo. Training with him for the 1966 competitions was rigorous, demanding and challenging, but the best thing that ever happened to her skating career. When Peggy discovered that he'd earned a degree in architecture, she began to understand why his mind thought in such precise terms. Better than anyone else she had known, he could see and show the exactness of school figures. Almost immediately, he found something wrong.

"Your turns, Peggy," he said. "They are not good. We shall make them so."

His Italian accent delighted Peggy, although she found it difficult to understand at first. But slowly she relaxed under his coaching methods and paced herself carefully, perfecting the turns and increasing her skating time to build up altitude stamina.

That was one of the super pluses about the move to Colorado. In the southern California area, as skating became increasingly popular, rink time became more scarce. She had to run from rink to rink, finding an hour of patch time here, an hour of patch time there, totally ruining her concentration. Once, she'd been so desperate Mom even called their old friend, Neil Rose, a rink operator in northern California to see if he had any open time.

Now at the Broadmoor, she could use the entire rink during her allotted ice time and, as in competition, lay out her figures undisturbed. Then, after skating indoors, she'd work on Colorado College's outdoor rink.

"You'll be skating outdoors at World's in Davos," Carlo said one day as they drove along a tree-lined street. "And it makes a big difference. You'll need more physical force, for one thing, to overcome skating against the wind. And the texture of outdoor ice must be experienced."

Peggy usually skated outdoors only on weekends, but in the weeks just before the Nationals competition, she skated her free style for an hour each evening after dinner. Although it could be bitterly cold at that time of night, she didn't mind. She loved the feeling of being totally alone for that hour, hearing only the whisper of her skates as they skimmed over the ice. Total concentration flowed from her brain to her blades without any stops along the way.

The weeks melted into one another for Peggy as she practiced and practiced. All other activities drifted out of her life and soon Peggy sadly realized she would have to make other arrangements for high school. She simply couldn't attend classes and skate too. Mom inquired and soon found the perfect solution. Peggy enrolled in Hollywood Professional High in California and studied by correspondence. Each Friday she mailed her homework back to Hollywood, appearing in person when it was time for final exams.

After flying back to Los Angeles for several choreography sessions with Bob Paul, Peggy felt ready for the Nationals in Berkeley at the end of January. Dad decided to go along and visit old friends in the bay area before the competition began.

Peggy felt confident but not cocky as she took a commanding lead in the school figures. On free-style night, she breezed through her performance, winning her third National Senior Ladies title. The training under Carlo had built her stamina, made her more consistent and given her a confidence she'd not experienced before. Tina Noyes placed second and Pamela Schneider from New Jersey finished third. Her friends, Ron and Cynthia Kauffman, won the Senior pairs again and would also represent the United States at the World's with her in February.

They returned to Colorado Springs immediately because there was so much to do. In the midst of preparations for the World's, Peggy accepted the Young American of the Month award on February 8. Then departure day arrived.

"Wish you were coming, too, Dad," Peggy said, as she closed her suitcase with a snap.

"Wish I were, too, honey." He looked out the window to admire the view of the mountains. "But I'll be there in my thoughts and heart. You know that."

Peggy turned to look at him. "I've got such a good feeling about this competition, Dad." She tried to sound cheerful, but for some reason, she hated to leave Dad this time. More than any other time, she didn't want to leave him now. "Dad, are you feeling all right?"

He turned to look at her. "All right?" His voice sounded hearty enough. "Of course, I feel all right. My daughter's about to become the world's figure-skating champion. I'm the happiest man in the world!"

He grabbed her suitcase and walked to the front door, where Mom was waiting. Peggy opened her purse one more time and looked inside. Yes, there it was, the green gum wrapper Greg had given her last night. For luck, he'd said. I hope it will bring all of us luck, she thought, and went out to catch the plane to Davos.

Some publicity pictures sent to fans.

(left) Peggy executing a spread
eagle. (right) Peggy at eighteen.

Peggy demonstrating a double loop.

This was taken in 1967 when Peggy was nineteen.

(left) Another publicity picture. (right) Peggy demonstrates the layback spin here.

A very happy Peggy being greeted at the airport by friends and fans after winning a world competition.

Peggy holds the Babe Didrikson Zaharias award which she received for being the most outstanding woman athlete of the year.

Peggy, after the 1968 Olympics, with a bronze statue of her doing the layback spin.

11

World Champion

Peggy and the other members of the U.S. World's team created interest from the press when they stepped off the plane at Davos wearing bluejeans and ten-gallon hats.

"Why the western wear?" a reporter asked Peggy.

"The Broadmoor Skating Club thought it would be fun for all of us to wear these hats." She pushed hers over one eye at a rakish angle. "People can more easily distinguish us at the World championships."

The team checked into the Belvedere Hotel with their chaperones and Peggy went to work at a nearby rink immediately. Although her attitude was positive and Carlo felt good about her chances, she was still the underdog. Petra Burka from Canada would be defending her title and she was a strong competitor and great skater.

Peggy knew that only four times in the history of the World's competition had a reigning champion been defeated, so the odds were against her. And there was also Gabrielle Seyfert of East Germany. She was European Ladies champion and considered a real contender. No, Peggy would have to work hard if she expected to win. Don't get too confident or you'll let down, she told herself. Work. Concentrate. That's the name of the game.

On Friday, the first two figures were skated by everyone and Peggy immediately took a sixteen-point lead. "I'm really surprised, Mom," she said at dinner. "I can't believe I'm leading."

"It must be the extra practice after we moved to Colorado Springs."

Next day, Peggy skated the final four figures and beat Petra in each one, leading by forty-nine points as compulsories were concluded. She felt tingly and shivery inside. She was so close now. Did she dare to think about winning the title? Did she dare think about it just a little bit? To be World's champion was something to be hoped for, dreamed about, but to actually become champion? She was about to have a super case of the nervous willies. Her stomach churned so crazily that she knew any food she put in it would bounce right out again. She found herself chewing her lower lip and made herself stop, for the moment at least.

Pamela Schneider came up to congratulate her in the hotel corridor. "No one can catch you now, Peggy," her teammate said. "Tomorrow the World!"

"Thanks, Pam," Peggy said. "Maybe, well, we'll see

what happens in free style. Hey, you're doing pretty great yourself. Eighth place is fantastic."

Pam walked down the hall to her room and Peggy shut the door to the room she shared with Mom. She felt restless and her nerves seemed tighter than laces on a pair of badly fitting skates. Although she should be in bed resting, sleep was out of the question for some time.

"Let's go shopping," Mom said to her and put down her sewing.

"Now?" Peggy asked. "The stores must be closed, Mom."

"I know," Mom replied. "Let's just go window shopping. Good for the nerves and great for the pocketbook."

They bundled up against the late-afternoon cold air and walked down the main street of Davos. Brightly lighted coffee shops lined the streets and Peggy looked inside to see people seated at tables. They were relaxed as they enjoyed conversation and laughter over their coffee and pastries. Further down the street, shop windows were filled with expensive ski clothes.

"I'd love to learn to ski sometime," Peggy remarked, already planning her wardrobe from the selection in front of her.

"No better place to learn than here," Mom said. "At least that's what people say. Maybe, after your competition days are over, you can take it up."

"But there's no law against watching now, is there?" Peggy said. "I've got a great idea. When World's is over, let's go up to Parsenn run and just watch for awhile. Can we, Mom?"

Their heads turned at the same time in the direction of

Parsenn funicular railway that went straight up the side of the snow-covered mountain to Weissflujock. Yes, Peggy thought, it would be fun to do the watching for a change instead of being watched all the time.

She looked at the clear sky. Not a cloud in it, just stars beginning to shine as the dusky twilight gave way to night. The weather should be clear tomorrow, she thought. No storms in sight. Then she turned in the other direction and saw the outline of the old Gothic church and the imposing city hall which dominated the town of twelve thousand. I love this town, she thought. Maybe I'll always remember it as my lucky town.

"Come on, Peggy. It's getting cold. We'd better go in."

The next morning, Peggy awoke to a room full of sunshine. She ran to the window and looked outside. Snow that had fallen several days ago glittered beneath the sun's rays, giving the view a brightness that Peggy could feel inside her as well. It's a beautiful day to skate, she thought, and hurried to get ready.

After dressing in a soft rose jersey dress with white ruffles at the cuffs and neck, Peggy pinned the green gum wrapper inside a sleeve. Then she went to the rink. The vast terrace surrounding it was crowded to capacity now. She'd read that five thousand people were expected and it looked like they'd all come. The draw was held and she placed seventeenth. After learning that Petra would skate in the eleventh position, Peggy found a quiet corner in which to wait.

She thought about her program and the new figure she would perform today for the first time. So much was riding on her performance now, that perhaps this was the wrong time to introduce anything new. If she won, it would mark a comeback for American skaters, who'd not figured in competition since the entire team was wiped out five years ago. Had it really been that long since the day she'd heard about Mr. Kipp and his kids? If anyone had told her then that she would be here now, at this moment, ready to skate for the championship of the world, she'd never have believed them. True, she'd dreamed about it, but to have a dream come true right before your very eyes is pretty spooky, she thought.

"Peggy, let's go," Carlo whispered.

She skated to the center of the rink and let the strains of Tchaikovsky's *Pathétique* slowly fill every cell in her body as she glided out into her opening move. How can anyone in this world get along without music, she thought. I can exist without everything else, but music. It transforms you into whatever you want to be, wherever you want to go, if you just let it pull you along on its wings of sound.

She felt as if she had wings now and leaped into the figure that she'd invented. It was a combination spread eagle, double axel, and it worked perfectly. Vaguely she heard applause from the audience as she continued. A double flip came next. Carlo said it was the hardest figure for her to do, but here she was in the World's doing it anyway. Think now, Peggy, she told herself. She stepped into a left inside edge. Her free leg was in front now and she pointed her toe, the free shoulder and right arm were back, the left arm in front. So far, so good, she thought and continued through the rest of the intricate maneuver.

Even that worked, she thought. Even my double flip made it! Wow, oh double wow for my double flip!

Now she was nearly finished. The music segued to Saint-Saëns and Peggy stroked into her final spin, feeling the air rush around her in a brisk vortex of its own. She stopped, bowed, the music ended. I think I did it, she thought. Oh gosh, I think I did it. I didn't miss one step, one figure, one jump.

Her lips trembled as she skated off, her eyes blinking back tears of relief and fatigue. As she reached the edge of the ice, people rushed her and she felt panicky. Where's Mom? Where's Carlo, she thought. Suddenly, she saw them as they pushed their way through the crowd. Carlo hugged her, then Mom held her closely for a moment.

"I did it all, I did my whole program," she said, tears streaming down her face.

"It was perfect, Peggy, just perfect," Carlo said. His face was split with the largest smile Peggy had ever seen.

"I'm speechless, honey," Mom said. "I never even dared to dream of this day."

They hugged each other again and Peggy thought, if only Dad could have been here, too. If only Dad . . . She longed to hear the sound of his voice. Maybe there would be time for a telephone call later.

In a couple of minutes the judges made it official, awarding her nine ordinal points and a complete score that overwhelmed Gaby Seyfert in second place by sixty-two points.

"Wow," Peggy said, letting out a long, relaxing sigh. "The big scare is over."

On the winner's platform, with her gold medal hanging

from a bright ribbon around her neck, she posed for photographers and answered questions.

"What did you think about while you were skating, Peggy?"

"What was your worst moment?"

"What was your best?"

"How does it feel to be seventeen and the figure-skating champion of the world?"

She fielded the reporters' questions neatly, answered quickly, yet thoroughly, until they were satisfied. As they drifted away, she located Mom and Carlo and Pam and some of the others.

"I'm hungry," she said, putting on her blade guards. "I wonder where I can find a piece of banana cream pie?"

In the days that followed, Peggy found herself whirling from press conference to practice sessions to exhibition performances, as she began the World tour sponsored by the International Skating Union. This was her third tour for them, and although it was hard work, the skaters had fun after the show. They went out together and danced in coffeehouses, shopped in out of-the-way places and ate as much of the luscious local food as their diets would allow.

Midway during the tour, Peggy flew to Boston alone for an exhibition benefit performance. Mom stayed with the tour in Europe because Peggy planned to fly back imme-diately after one show. It seemed strange to be alone and she felt vaguely adrift without a member of the family around. She came off the ice to enthusiastic applause and someone hurried up with a bouquet of deep-red roses. She returned to the rink for another bow, then started down the hall to her dressing room.

The dark figure in the shadows startled her at first,

then slowly her eyes became accustomed to the dimness and she stared unbelievingly. It couldn't be. It just couldn't be. Was she awake or dreaming? She had to be awake, she could feel herself trembling with emotion.

"Dad," she cried, running as fast as he blade guards would allow. "Dad, oh, Dad, let me look at you." She threw her arms around him, scattering roses everywhere. Then she stood back to look at his face. He looked tired, there were lines on his face she hadn't noticed before. But that was understandable. He must have driven long hours to get there.

"Oh, Dad, I'm so glad to see you. When did you come? How long can you stay? How do you feel? How are the kids? Have you seen Greg?"

Dad started to laugh. "Whoa. Slow down, Peggy. Which question shall I answer first?"

"Oh, I don't know. I don't care." Peggy started to cry. "I'm so happy to see you."

They walked slowly toward her dressing room. Dad said, "When Mom wrote that you'd be here, I just had to come. By the way, I accepted an award for you from radio station KOA. You were voted Athlete of the Month."

"That's nice," Peggy said. "Did you drive all the way? Didn't that wear you out?"

"Yes, I drove, Peggy, and I feel just fine. I'm going to interrupt the return trip a little by stopping in Cleveland and working for a few weeks at the *Plain Dealer*. I can visit with our friends at the same time."

"Oh, that will be great, Dad, but I wish you didn't have to work at all."

"They need me, Peggy, and it will be like a paid

vacation anyway. I have so much fun seeing the people in Cleveland."

The next day, Peggy flew back to Europe to join the tour. She waved good-bye to Dad at the airport, feeling depressed and overcome with homesickness. Being a champion had compensations, but it also had limitations. When she got back to Colorado Springs with all her family and Greg, no one would be able to pry her away for a long long time.

When the tour arrived in Russia, Peggy enjoyed learning about the country through her friends, the Protopopovs, who were again on the tour. After they finished the Moscow exhibition, Mom called the American embassy to see if there were any messages for them. There were none.

"Ready, Peggy?" Mom said. "It's time to go to the airport. I'm anxious to go to Germany now, aren't you?"

"Yes, because it means we're that much closer to home."

They arrived at the bustling Moscow International to wait for their flight. Mom seemed unusually restless, Peggy thought, watching her as she walked aimlessly about.

Just then a man walked up to Mom and began talking to her. As Peggy watched, Mom suddenly put her hands to her face. What could be wrong? Peggy rushed to Mom's side.

"What's the matter, Mom? What's happened?"

Suddenly Peggy didn't want to know. She wanted to scream "Stop! Don't tell me. If you don't say the words, then it can't have happened."

"I'm from the American Embassy," the man was saying to her. "After your mother called this afternoon, we received a message and have been trying to find you before you left the country."

"Oh, Peggy," Mom said. The words sounded like a moan coming from a deep place inside her. "Your Dad, honey. He's dead."

Peggy heard the words and tried not to believe them, but she couldn't put herself off. Dad was dead. She knew it, because she felt so lost and empty that she must be only a shell of some kind standing there. Slowly, her whole body took the blow, as if someone had thrown her a physical punch that left her out of breath and numb. She and Mom looked at one another without seeing.

"Let's go home," Peggy said through lips that were wooden. "Let's go home."

12

Life Without Dad

*P*eggy and Mom took the next flight after learning from the embassy that Dad had his second and fatal heart attack in Cleveland. There he had died on April 6. At least he was with his friends, Peggy thought. She and Mom seemed to cry all the way home.

The family gathered in Colorado Springs for the funeral and Peggy was grateful that Uncle George and Aunt Ellen and the rest of them were there to help Mom. She and her sisters felt as if they'd been caught up in a terrible storm, then set suddenly adrift. They would have been no help at all. Several days later, after everyone had left, Mom called the girls together.

"Time for a family conference," she said, and for a

moment, no one spoke. It was as if they were waiting for Dad to join them.

"We have to make plans for our future," Mom began. "Peggy has won the World's championship. Maybe she should retire now. After all, she's proven what she can do."

While Peggy waited to hear what her sisters would say, she thought, I'm so glad that Dad knew I won World's. He was so positive I would. It was as if he were waiting for that one competition before . . . she couldn't finish the thought. Tears pooled quickly in her eyes and she looked out the window toward the mountains.

"Peggy," Maxine was calling her. "Don't you want to go on to the Olympics? That's less than two years away."

"That's right, Maxine," Mom said. "It is, and if we tighten the budget, we'll get along just fine on Dad's insurance and Social Security."

"No," Peggy blurted out, "it isn't right. I can't ask you girls to make anymore sacrifices for me."

"But that's just it," Janice said. "We haven't made any sacrifices. You only sacrifice when you give up something. I haven't given up anything. I'm doing what I've always wanted to do. Nurse's training is the greatest thing that ever happened to me."

"And I'm president of the ski club at school," Maxine said. "I'd never have put on a pair of skis if we hadn't moved here so you could train."

"Please don't quit, Peggy," Cathy said. The words slipped out so plaintively that Peggy knew they had to be the sincerest words she'd ever heard.

"It's agreed then," Janice said.

"Absolutely," Maxine said. "I want Peggy to win a gold medal at the Olympics."

"Your sisters sound pretty positive." Mom smiled at Peggy.

"I won't let them down," Peggy assured her.

Peggy took a brief vacation from the ice to study hard before graduating from Hollywood Professional High School in June. It was a time too, when Peggy and her family grew closer together as they adjusted to life without Dad. The smallest details were the hardest. Setting the table for five instead of six and not listening for his familiar footsteps and warm hello when he came in from work at the end of a day were two habits that were difficult to change.

Greg Jenkins's presence helped Peggy and her family ease through the worst days. He mowed the lawn and ran errands. He became a big brother to her sisters, sometimes helping with homework. Peggy saw how understanding and kind he was and her admiration for him grew in one giant leap.

Peggy and Greg enjoyed being together, bicycling along the shady streets of town, improving their tennis, and swimming and picnicking. Sometimes they even skated together. The days and weeks were full of activity because Peggy could never be still even while on vacation, but it was the kind of activity that helped her relax from the demands of competition skating.

"What are you going to do when you graduate?" Greg asked one day as they rode a tandem bike around town.

"I have a tour this summer and then I'll go into training for the Nationals."

"I'm talking about your education, Peggy," Greg said. Have you thought anymore about college?"

"Yes. I'm thinking about Colorado College, especially. I need a degree to teach school."

"Hey, that's neat. When did you decide to become a schoolteacher?"

"I don't really remember ever deciding one day that's what I'd become. It's just something I've thought about since I was a little girl."

They pedaled on in silence for a block or two.

"I've always liked working with little kids," Peggy said. "You know, like at Sunday School or helping them at the rink. I think I'd like teaching kindergarten or first grade best of all."

"You've probably already taught a lot of kids that age without really knowing it," Greg said.

"How?"

"By being what you are, a clean-cut, all-American type, who's shown what talent and hard work can do. When those little kids come up to you at the rink and ask for your autograph, they do it because you've given them something to work for. Maybe one day they can be a champion like you."

"Greg, that's so beautiful." Peggy turned to look at him. As she did so, she turned the handlebars sharply and nearly upset their tandem.

"Hey, don't let all that praise and admiration go to your head," Greg laughed as he managed to keep them from falling.

Later that summer, Peggy joined the ISU tour, skating in the United States, Canada and Europe. European newspapers began to talk of her as "America's shy Bambi" and tried to link her romantically with many of the top athletes in the countries she was visiting. When she saw her picture in a newspaper with someone she'd never met, it puzzled her at first.

"How do they do this, Mom?" she asked.

Mom answered, "They cut out pictures of each of you, put them together and then photograph the pictures as if you were standing side by side."

"But why do they go to all that trouble?"

"You know how interested the Europeans are in figure skating," Mom said. "They love to read stories about the top skaters, so the newspapers print as much as they can about you and the others. Sometimes they stretch it just a little."

After that, Peggy laughed when she was pictured with a boy she barely knew and once she even sent the newspaper clipping home to Greg.

Peggy remembered her mother's words about the Europeans' interest in figure skating when they went to Dresden, East Germany, to skate in an exhibition at an outside rink. Clouds gathered shortly after their arrival, then a heavy rain began to fall with a steady, insistent rhythm. Surely we won't skate, Peggy thought, as they sat in a bus, waiting for a decision to be made. Even as they waited, the audience continued to arrive, huddling beneath umbrellas or whatever shelter they could find. Thousands of people sat patiently, and after several hours the officials announced that the exhibition would go on as scheduled! Peggy and the other skaters went out to the rink and gave the performances of their lives. Despite the discomfort of having her hair plastered to her face and being soaked all the way through to her bootlaces, Peggy could never have been happier. When audiences were that devoted to her sport, she responded from her heart.

That fall Peggy entered Colorado College taking an education course and modern dance from Norman Cornick. Now her practice time with Carlo increased to six hours a day as she prepared for the Nationals in January. Each day she warmed up meticulously, skating slow, simple circles, then gradually working into the school figures, practicing as much as half an hour on each figure. Sometimes it took her a week of practice to get through the entire set.

She continued to use the outdoor rink at Colorado College when it was available. Maxine occasionally came with her.

"I really like your company," Peggy said as she drove through cold and empty streets.

"Thanks," Maxine said, smothering a yawn. "I don't have anything else to do at five o'clock in the morning, so I might as well change your records on the PA system."

Peggy smiled, knowing this was Maxine's way of saying she wanted to help in any way she could. "I hope you brought plenty of hot chocolate in that thermos," she said.

"I hope I did, too," Maxine said, leaning back and closing her eyes. "Wake me when we get there."

Peggy drove on through the dark, quiet city, aware of how much her family's continued support meant to her.

In mid-January, Peggy flew to Omaha and the Nationals competition began. She completely dominated the compulsories. Going into the free-style event on Saturday evening, January 18, she led Tina Noyes in second place and Jennie Walsh from Torrance, California, in third. That night, dressed in a gossamer gold costume, with a matching ribbon to hold back her hair, she performed her program expertly, although she knew it was not an inspired performance. Something was missing from it that she couldn't quite explain. Perhaps knowing this was the first competition she'd skated that Dad hadn't been involved in held her back emotionally. Whatever it was, she skated well enough to win, but that was all.

Then Jennie Walsh, a new skater at the Nationals level, came out to skate and electrified everyone with her combinations of loops and spins. She returned to the rink for an almost unprecedented encore and Peggy clapped harder than anyone else for the young competitor. I've got to recapture that feeling of inspiration, Peggy thought.

She won the North American Ladies title in Montreal in early February, then flew to Vienna for the World's competition. Peggy moved into an early eight-point lead on Tuesday, February 28, after skating the first compulsory, an inside counter, although stiff competition came from Valerie Jones of Canada. The Protopopovs won the Senior pairs competition that evening and Peggy thrilled to her friends' flawless skating. On Wednesday, Peggy skated two more figures, a left outside rocker and a right forward paragraph double three, and increased her lead. By Thursday, after the final figure was skated, she was twenty points ahead of Gaby Seyfert of East Germany and sixty-nine points ahead of Valerie Jones.

On Saturday evening Peggy, dressed in shocking-pink

jersey, waited tensely in the dressing room of the Vienna Ice Club. Then her name was called and she skated out to tremendous applause. It's so hard to skate up to everyone's expectations, she thought, as her music began.

Thirty seconds into her program, she noticed her timing was several beats off the pace. Moving into her double axel, she hurried the jump. She lost her balance and came down hard on the seat of her pants, sliding into the wall. Her hands, scraping across the ice, felt hot against the cold surface. The audience gasped as she took the blow, but she ignored the noise, her festering thoughts of rage against herself and the throbbing spot where she'd landed. She picked herself up quickly. Stay cool, she thought.

Easing back into the routine, she finished with a series of double toe loops, a double flip and blended a flying camel into a double lutz. A second double axel came next. Should she try it again? Everyone knew it was in her program. She'd better do it or people would think she was chicken. She leaped into it and it worked beautifully. Her music ended and she skated off to a standing ovation.

When Carlo came up to her, she said, "I wish I could go out and do the whole thing over, and this time I wouldn't make a mistake."

She won her second World's championship ninety-four points ahead of Gaby Seyfert in second place. Standing on the winner's platform to receive her gold medal, Peggy thought that this hadn't been her best year for performance. Next year, she thought, I've got to do better.

13

Olympics, 1968

*W*hen Peggy returned from the World's competition and the ISU tour, she didn't experience the normal let-down feeling that usually accompanied the end of a skating season. Rather, she felt tense, as if ready to pounce or spring at anything that moved. She knew what was bothering her, of course. It was the Olympics, just six months away, that filled her every waking thought. And her nights, too. Sometimes she dreamed about it. Awake or asleep, she couldn't seem to get away from it.

After a short break, she resumed her practice schedule and it seemed that she'd been preparing for this one event all her life. Oh, she'd worked toward this title or that one as she moved up in competition, but in the back of her mind there'd always been the feeling that one day she'd have a real chance at the Olympics. Innsbruck had been another stepping stone, just like Squaw Valley and Cleveland and Davos, to this Olympics.

Even the times she'd talked about quitting had only strengthened her resolve to win a gold medal. Each time of hesitation had been followed by a stronger determination to succeed.

One afternoon, as Peggy neared the end of a practice session, she skated to the edge of the rink. As she rubbed her throbbing calf muscles, she suddenly noticed how damp and sticky she felt from the exertion of the last couple of hours. When someone skated by and she started to say hello, her mouth was so dry it felt glued shut and she could only wave. Sometimes I wonder if it's really worth it, she thought, trying to psych herself up for another hour's work.

Cathy suddenly appeared, walking along the spectators' aisle.

"What's up?" Peggy managed to say around the seeming bale of cotton in her mouth.

"Nothing much," Cathy replied. She leaned against the railing that circled the rink. "Except Mom thought you'd get a big kick out of this letter that came this afternoon."

Peggy turned the envelope over in her hands. It was addressed to "Miss Peggy Fleming, U.S.A." Eagerly she opened it, but couldn't read a word except her name. Cathy looked over her shoulder.

"What language is that?"

"Looks like German," Peggy said, still trying to make out the words. "Look, I think that says Vienna."

"Probably someone saw you at World's and wanted to tell you what a rotten skater you are." Cathy ducked as Peggy took a mock swing at her.

"Take this home for me, will you, Cathy?" Peggy returned the letter to her. "I want to show it to my grandchildren one day. And thanks for bringing it over."

Suddenly her muscles stopped aching, she felt cool and relaxed and ready to tear into her compulsories again. Miss Peggy Fleming, U.S.A. That letter had found her, out of all the millions of people in this country, it had come right to her mailbox. Someone cared enough to write it and lots of people cared along the way to find out where she lived. She began to circle the ice in forward crossovers, gaining speed and feeling the air whip her face. Worth it? Was all the practice and hard work worth it? You better believe it, she thought.

Over the next months, the days settled into neat and tidy patterns as Peggy practiced, met with Carlo for extra lessons, studied at Colorado College and saw Greg every weekend. Only a few times was the pattern broken, when she flew to Los Angeles for extra choreography sessions with Bob Paul. And then it was January and time to go to Philadelphia for the Nationals.

The night before she left, Peggy walked with Greg in the crisp wintry air.

"This is for you, Peggy," Greg said. They stopped and he put something in the palm of her furry mitten.

"My green gum wrapper," Peggy said, as they started walking again. "Oh, Greg, I was afraid you'd forget."

"No way, but this is the third one, Peg." Greg began to laugh. "I can barely keep up with you."

"You don't have to chew much longer." Peggy giggled as she said that. Then slowly, very thoughtfully, she added, "I think this will be the last gum wrapper I'll need."

Greg stopped to look at her and she tried to see his face in the gathering darkness. "Do you mean what I think you mean, Peggy? You're going to quit after Olympics and World's?"

"I'll be twenty in July," she said. "I've been skating in amateur competitions for nearly eleven years. I figured out that amounts to about twenty thousand hours of practice time on the ice. I think it's time, don't you?"

The ice at the Spectrum in Philadelphia was tricky, but Peggy kept a cool head and maintained a firm control over her tracings. At the end of compulsories, she moved far ahead of the others. On Friday evening, she watched Cynthia and Ron Kauffman skate in the pairs free style. They maneuvered through their intricate program, which included a double slip twist, a one-arm overhaul, a satellite spin, and wound up with the guillotine in which Ron spun and kicked his foot over Cynthia's head. Peggy was breathless as they finished to a standing ovation.

"Have you ever seen such skating?" Peggy asked Mom as they hurried back to their hotel.

On Saturday evening it was Peggy's turn. She pinned the green gum wrapper to her costume, then skated with a confidence she'd never felt before. Her timing, her elevation, her spins worked perfectly for her. Evidently the judges thought so, too, because they each gave her a 5.9 for technical method. In interpretation and style, two of the judges gave her the full six points allowed for perfection, while the others gave her 5.9s. She won her fifth straight Nationals title, with Tina Noyes placing second and Janet Lynn from Rockford, Illinois, third.

"That was one of the greatest performances ever given by a woman in Nationals competition," a telelvision reporter said into his mike as he stopped her before glaring lights for an interview. "The Olympics ought to be a breeze for you, Peggy."

"Thank you." She smiled weakly and hurried back to her dressing room. If only people knew how much pressure they applied when they said things like that, she thought. If only people knew what it feels like knowing you're expected to be perfect all the time. Suddenly her confidence drained from her. Losing is a luxury that I can't afford anymore, she thought. She had a feeling that she wouldn't really relax again, until all competition was truly over for her.

A couple of weeks later, Peggy and Mom reached Grenoble, France, early enough for Peggy to get in some practice time before the opening ceremonies began and for Mom to sew one costume after another until she finally felt satisfied.

"What do you think, Peggy?" she asked, holding up the pale green jersey trimmed with rhinestones. "Isn't this the one for free style?"

"That's beautiful, Mom," Peggy said. "You're right, that's the one."

On February 6, President Charles de Gaulle of France, a hatless figure towering above the crowd, stood in the presidential box and watched with the other spectators as the athletes from thirty-seven nations paraded into the stadium. Peggy proudly marched in the one-hundred-thirteen-member delegation from the United States behind Terry McDermott, a former gold-medal winner, who carried the flag.

The nine cannons boomed through the Isère Valley at five-second intervals to mark the arrival of the Olympic flame in the stadium. For Peggy, this was one of the most inspiring moments of the Games. When that flame leaped high against the sky, her heart leaped right along with it. She was back once more at the Olympics and the thrill and excitement were just as real and meaningful to her as the first time.

After the mass singing of the Olympic hymn, she paraded with the others to waiting buses to be transported back to the Olympic village. During the ride, she heard about Cynthia Kauffman's fall when she and her brother were practicing earlier that day. Cynthia had injured her left wrist and although they were continuing in competition, Peggy knew how difficult it would be for her to perform. She felt depressed for her friends.

Later that day, Peggy realized that many competitors in her dorm, including roommate Janet Lynn, were coming down with a virus that sounded all too familiar. The old sore-throat number again, she thought. When Mom learned of it, she suggested a daring move.

"Leave the village and move into the hotel with me," she urged. "You owe it to yourself, Peggy, to stay as healthy as possible now. You've got enough pressure on you as it is."

Peggy hesitated only for a moment. Mom was right

and Peggy quickly settled in with her, although there was much talk throughout the village about this unusual action.

On Wednesday Peggy skated the first two of her compulsories, a paragraph three backward on the left foot and an inside rocker on the right, and immediately piled up a thirty-point lead over Gaby Seyfert of East Germany.

"Peggy is practically unbeatable," Gaby's mother said to Mom as Peggy walked by.

Gosh, Peggy thought, feeling the pressure continue to build. I wish I hadn't heard that.

The next day, Peggy traced nearly perfect patterns on the final three figures and increased her lead over Gaby by seventy-seven points. All nine judges gave her their first-place ordinal points. A reporter cornered her as she headed back to the hotel.

"You're a shoo in, Peggy," he said. "Gonna play it safe in free style? You can win, you know, by just showing up."

Peggy's temper flared slightly. "What kind of champion would I be then?" she asked. "My dad taught me to always do my best. Tomorrow night, I'm going to give it all I've got."

Slowly ever so slowly, Peggy's thoughts drifted back to now, to the present moment. Suddenly there were no more tomorrows. Tomorrow night was here. Slowly she returned to this moment all the others in her life had been building toward. That expression she'd heard or read somewhere certainly fit now. What was it? Oh yes, "All the past is prologue." So right, so right.

And now it was nearly time. She rose from the chair and slipped into her pale green jersey dress, checking carefully to make sure the gum wrapper was secure. Her boots were laced correctly, her hair seemed in place after a final pass with the spray can. She applied more lipstick. It helped to have all these things to do in a tidy and orderly fashion, one after the other. That way, she couldn't think about her program, her music or the people. Oh, yes, people. Better try the cabbage routine tonight, she thought. Yes, the cabbages would definitely be there in row number one tonight. She felt like a teakettle whose lid was about to blow off. Her temples throbbed, her lips felt parched and her hands clammy.

A knock sounded on the door. "You're next, Peggy," someone said. She looked at herself in the mirror. Okay, she thought. Let's go. She thumped to the door and opened it. She walked down the hall to the rink. Carlo stood rinkside, his dark eyes gleaming. Somewhere in the stadium, her mother watched and waited. Her friends were watching and waiting, too. Bob Paul was there. So was Bill Udell, from California. And Cynthia and Ron and Gaby and Tina and Janet and the Protopopovs. All waiting.

Carlo held out his hand for her blade guards. "Good luck," he whispered. As she stepped to the ice she accidentally caught the rhinestone trim of her skating dress on her tights. Terrific, she thought, as she shook it loose. I may do a strip before I do a spin.

She skated to the center of the ice and now she was completely alone in the midst of thousands of people. The familiar, haunting melody of Tschaikovsky's *Pathétique* symphony floated out to greet her and she moved into its sound, feeling it envelop her, then take control. Gracefully, she glided into two double loops and followed with a double axel. So far, so good, she thought, although that axel could have been better.

As the music segued into the *Romeo and Juliet* Overture, she floated with it into a back spiral. Both arms stretched in front of her now in a perfect balletic position. Ballet seemed so natural now, she couldn't imagine how she'd skated without the classical movements before. She glided into a layback spin, bending far back with her arms circled in front of her. As she moved into more loops and splits and a double lutz, her music changed to Saint-Saëns's *Samson and Delilah.* The air brushed her cheeks as the music lifted her out of herself, and she existed now only in some unknown, timeless spot. She felt her body leaping, spinning, skimming, floating across the ice, yet did not feel a part of it.

How long had she been skating? Minutes, days, weeks, years? She really didn't know. The music reminded her, it prodded her and she stroked into the most difficult combination, the spread eagle, double axel. Then she whirled into a scratch spin and suddenly the four longest minutes of her life were over. Bowing, she let the cheering and applause embrace her for one long, delirious, wonderful moment. She warmed herself in the love that she could feel reaching out to her from every person there.

And then she thought her heart would burst inside.

Her lips began to tremble, her eyes filled and suddenly she couldn't see. Here I go with the crying scene again, she thought, letting the tears stream unchecked. The whole world is watching me cry.

She skated off to Mom's and Carlo's outstretched arms. She buried her head on Mom's shoulders and said, "It's so good to have it over." Then slowly, she drew a deep breath and exhaled, as though it were the very first time she'd ever breathed.

"We're all so proud of you," Mom managed to say through her own tears. Carlo hugged her fiercely, then ducked away to hide his emotions.

Cameras blinked at her, microphones waited expectantly, hot television lights threatened to melt her. People, sincere in their feelings, rushed up to hug and kiss her until she felt like a rag doll whose stuffing is about to spill out. Somehow she got through the questions and answers as she waited for her score.

Finally it came. She received 5.9 for artistic quality from each judge and 5.9 from all judges but three for technical quality. Peggy won eighty-eight points ahead of Gaby. Hana Maskova of Czechoslovakia finished third and Tina was fourth.

Then Peggy stepped out on the ice to the winner's platform to receive the Olympic gold medal. Hana stood on one side of her and Gaby on the other. Although the medal was heavy as it hung from a ribbon around her neck, she felt an enormous weight had been lifted from her shoulders. Suddenly Peggy felt like the inside of a bottle of champagne. She couldn't stop smiling and laughing and waving.

"How do you like my new little necklace?" she asked of no one in particular.

Then the band began to play the "Star-Spangled Banner" and she nearly cried again. No one can ever know this feeling, unless she's standing here, Peggy thought. I'll never be able to tell anyone how I feel. I just hope that other girls like me can experience it one day.

As the final strains of the national anthem dissolved into silence, Peggy finally got the message. She'd done it, what she started out to do so many years ago. With Mom's and Dad's encouraging love, her sisters' support, her coaches' instructions and her own hard work, she had turned this dream into reality. She really was an Olympic champion. Her name would go down in the record books for 1968 and for all time. Peggy Gale Fleming, U.S.A. Champion.

Epilogue

After Peggy won her third World's championship on Sunday, March 2, 1968, in Geneva, Switzerland, she flew home to the United States to receive the honors and tributes waiting for her.

On March 27, President Lyndon B. Johnson honored her with a reception in the White House Rose Garden. He thanked Peggy for "helping us with the gold drain by bringing back the gold medal." Then he picked a magnolia blossom and pinned it on Peggy's jacket. After they returned to his office, the President congratulated her once again for being the kind of a champion of whom her country could be so proud.

The following day she flew to Denver, where her plane was met by the governor of the state and the mayor of the city. A special plane then flew her to Colorado Springs where "Peggy Fleming Day" was proclaimed. Taking her place in a special gold convertible, she rode at the head of a motorcade through downtown, where tens of thousands cheered as she passed.

The parade ended at the Broadmoor World Arena, where a standing ovation greeted her as she entered to receive gifts and acknowledge speeches in her honor. Then, as a special thank you to all her friends there, she skated her favorite exhibition numbers to the music of *Ave Maria* and *West Side Story*.

On April 3, in New York City, she announced her retirement from amateur competition and signed a contract with Bob Banner Productions and the National Broadcasting Company. Since then she has appeared in six television specials, made many commercials and guest appearances, served as commentator at the 1972 Olympics, toured with the Ice Follies for four seasons and in her own ice show, "Concert on Ice" for several more. Peggy continues to guest star in "Holiday on Ice," the Ice Follies and returns to the White House frequently as a guest at state dinners for foreign dignitaries.

On June 13, 1970, Peggy married Dr. Gregory Jenkins in Los Angeles, California. They have one son, Andrew Thomas, born in 1977. The family now lives in Atherton, California, a suburb of San Francisco.

On June 10, 1975, Peggy was inducted into the Skating Hall of Fame, the youngest skater ever to be so honored for her extraordinary contribution to the world of figure skating. It is a fitting tribute to the talents and achievements of Miss Peggy Fleming, U.S.A. Champion.

Index